Demythologizing the Inner-City Child

Robert C. Granger and James C. Young, Editors
Georgia State University

The National Association for the Education of Young Children
Washington, D.C.

Cover Design by Rubin Krassner, Silver Spring, Maryland.

National Association for the Education of Young Children
1834 Connecticut Avenue, N.W.
Washington, DC 20009

Library of Congress Catalog Card Number: 76-47135

ISBN Catalog Number: 0-912674-50-4

Printed in the United States of America.

Table of Contents

Introduction

On March 25, 26, and 27, 1976, the Urban Life Foundation of Georgia State University sponsored a conference entitled *Demythologizing the Inner-City Child.* The conference solicited papers and symposia on the sociology, psychology, and education of inner-city children. This book of readings contains a selection of the papers presented at that conference.

The title of this book and the conference represents a concern that we, the conference designers and directors, have regarding the existing literature on inner-city children. *Demythologizing* refers to a concern that many myths or stereotypes have developed about the psychology, sociology, or education of inner-city children. Such myths as *inner-city children are linguistically deprived* or *inner-city children are culturally deprived* have been particularly powerful in determining interaction programs. Our position is that most of these myths are a result of ethnocentric paradigms for research which include a priori assumptions about the one right way to behave, speak, or raise one's children. The conference was conceived as a forum for the examination of extant myths surrounding inner-city children. Accordingly, papers or research approaching inner-city children from a relativistic or cultural difference, rather than a cultural deficit, paradigm were strongly encouraged.

The term *inner-city child* is also a conscious choice. By *inner-city* we refer to two features which give the term special social meaning: the groups that inhabit the inner cities of the United States, and the fact that the inner city is a product of forces external to itself. The inner-city child therefore may be defined as an individual member of a particular group whose members have, for a variety of reasons, been circumscribed to live there. This definition also implies that lives of residents of the inner city may be characterized by externally limited modes of interaction and mobility. Inner city, therefore, is not strictly a demographic term and inner-city children are not all children who live within central city geographic boundaries. Rather, they are children representing all shades of black, white, brown, red, and yellow who are ghettoized.

The chapters in this book address a variety of issues and myths. We have chosen to include a balance of empirical and expository selections to illustrate current research strategies and positions regarding existing literature. The readings are appropriate for persons working with inner-city children, policymakers, university personnel, students, and research workers.

We would like to acknowledge the assistance of many persons who aided in the presentation of the conference and the publication of this book of readings. First, we would like to thank the presenters at the conference and those who attended the conference. Many high quality presentations occurred which for reasons of cost and a variety of other factors could not be included in this book. At the end of the book we have included a complete conference listing with names, addresses, and paper titles of those papers presented. We encourage interested parties to write individual authors for papers of interest.

Second, we would like to thank our graduate assistants, Carol Shuford, Lois Clark, and Roma Klimczuk. These women aided us immeasurably in conference planning, implementation, and evaluation.

Third, we would like to acknowledge the assistance of the staff of the National Association for the Education of Young Children. Their professional expertise and support have been instrumental in bringing about this publication.

Robert C. Granger and James C. Young
Department of Early Childhood Education
Georgia State University

Cultural Pluralism and Myths

This first section is the most heterogeneous of the five sections in the book. The conceptual thread integrating the three chapters is the concern for issues fundamental to the positions of demythologizing and cultural pluralism. Fittingly, the section begins and ends with explicit references to W.E.B. Du Bois. Perhaps more than any other figure, Du Bois articulated the strength of and necessity for cultural pluralism.

Thomas Schmitz presents a clear exposition of the evolution of Du Bois's position and illustrates persuasively that the problems facing the inner-city child are caused by forces of White racism and classism.

Russell Irvine's examination of the implications of the conference title helps couch Du Bois's position in an important context. That is, Irvine illustrates that myths and the imposition of myths are not necessarily the result of a conscious act or some conspiratorial plot by the ruling power group. We agree that such an analysis would be simplistic. As Irvine notes, one does not need to develop a conspiratorial model of American society to realize that benefits are derived by those in power as myths and their imposition render the subordinate groups less powerful.

This focus upon the nature and function of myths in our society is also central to Asa Hilliard's chapter. In this far-ranging chapter Hilliard delimits not only existing myths but delineates characteristics of the mythmakers. This delineation provides an operational definition of the White racism discussed by Schmitz and further expands on the utility of myths for mythmakers described by Irvine.

Thomas Francis Schmitz

The Educational Theory of W.E.B. Du Bois: A Culturally Pluralistic Alternative

The life of William Edward Burghardt Du Bois spanned nearly a century, ninety-five of the most critical years of the Black American revolution. Born the year after the institution of southern reconstruction, Dr. Du Bois died on the eve of the 1963 March on Washington. Variously a scholar, poet, candidate for political office, theoretician, characterized as a "seer" and an "enigma," Du Bois was first, last, and always a *teacher*. Nearly all of his works—editorials, novels, volumes of poetry, autobiographies— are principally pedagogical in which he, aspiring to be the "selfless seeker of truth," attempted to explain the Black man in America, at first to the White race and then later to the Black race.

But to those who take the time to delve into the life of the man, he emerges as a much less paradoxical or enigmatic figure than he is commonly portrayed. And, as such, he is a much more manageable subject for scholarly inquiry and as a model for emulation. He emerges as a Black American forever conscious of "his two-ness,—an American, a Negro; two souls, two thoughts, two unreconciled strivings; two warring ideals in one dark body, whose dogged strength alone keeps it from being torn asunder" (Du Bois 1969, p. 45).

His New England, White, liberal upbringing thoroughly immersed the young scholar in the Protestant ethos of his day. He was without Black companions in early childhood and attended all White schools where he diligently and deliberately outpaced fellow students. It was in this early educational process that Du Bois found his forté. The young scholar received much well-deserved praise. Education, scholarly inquiry, and the pursuit of the truth unlocked the secrets of life itself and served him as a means to achieve acceptance and acclaim. Education was more than a means to an end, more than mere training for a vocation in life. It was, in Du Bois's mind, synonymous with life. Education studied life and life itself was basically pedagogical.

He perceived in his educational process at Fisk, and later at Harvard, a remedy to his own personal needs and to the needs of his race. At Fisk, he encountered for the first time large numbers of Black scholars and began the love affair with Black people that was to permeate and drive his life. His summers, spent as a teacher in the poverty-stricken backwoods schools of Wilson County, Tennessee, fulfilled a great personal need and dedicated him to the role of teacher. At Harvard he was accepted by White scholars such as William James, Josiah Royce, and Santayana as a fellow scholar and intellectual. In addition to the knowledge acquired, he also absorbed much of the Social Darwinism of his day. Early writings of encounters with members of his race are filled with poetic images of "Life behind the Veil" and romantic allusions to men and women of "caramel," "golden," and "mahogany" hues.

It should come as no particular surprise that he should envision liberal education as the means by which the Black race, stripped of all "culture" by two hundred years of chattel slavery and thirty years of economic bondage in his mind, could be regenerated. The Black race, or at least that segment of it that Du Bois had encountered during his pedagogical forays into the hollows of Tennessee, lacked the basic rudiments of a life acceptable to a young New England liberal. And they must have seemed incapable of generating those rudimentary tenets from their position of economic and social degradation. To Du Bois, what was required were more people like himself, dedicated and educated, "broad-minded, cultured men and women, to scatter civilization among a people whose ignorance was not simply of letters, but of life itself" (Du Bois 1969, p. 129). He called this educated elite his "missionaries of culture" (1969, p. 195), the Talented Tenth: "Progress in human affairs is more often a pull than a push, a surging forward of the exceptional man, and the lifting of his duller brethren slowly and painfully to his vantage ground" (1969, p. 127). Southern Whites would not provide the teachers necessary for the task, therefore, the Black race must provide them. Black institutions of higher education, such as Fisk and Spelman and Atlanta must "furnish the black world with adequate standards of human culture and lofty ideals of life" (Du Bois 1969, p. 129).

In 1905 Du Bois stated:

The function of the Negro college, then, is clear: it must maintain the standards of popular education, it must seek the social regeneration of the Negro, and it must help in the solution of the problems of race contact and cooperation. And finally, beyond all this, it must develop men. (Du Bois 1969, p. 138)

It is against this early model for Black higher education that Du Bois's controversy with Booker T. Washington and the Tuskegee Machine must be perceived. Du Bois thought Booker T. Washington's education compromise unnecessarily narrow. It provided an education for Black youth, but an education that was predicated upon submission to the dominant White power structure in three critical areas, by eschewing political power, by refusing to insist upon constitutionally guaranteed civil rights, and by relinquishing any claims to higher education.

In this early opposition to Washington's conciliation of the White South we see the seeds of the constitutionalism of Du Bois's educational theory. He demanded that an educational model for Black youth must not fail to insist upon the political and civil rights of its students. Black youth must be made to perceive their place in the American social structure. The truth must be taught. The truth, as Du Bois saw it, was that the Constitution of the United States guaranteed universal manhood suffrage, the right to due process of law, and outlawed slavery. The facts of the situation of the Black race in America, and particularly in the South, were that the White power structure had, through intimidation and overt violence, imposed caste restrictions upon the Black race. Booker T. Washington's acquiescence repudiated Negro claims to certain inalienable rights, the right to life, the right to liberty, and the right to pursue happiness. As Du Bois later stated, "The object of all true education is not to make men carpenters, but to make carpenters men" [Du Bois (1912) 1972 p. 120].

Du Bois conducted a lengthy research project on the Philadelphia Negro, became a professor at Atlanta University, headed the Niagara Movement, became Director of Publications and Research for the National Association for the Advancement of Colored People (NAACP), and edited *Crisis* magazine. In each of these capacities he perceived his role primarily as that of a theorist, a teacher leading his people in their struggle for desegregation.

During the twenties his enthusiasm for the Black race continually increased. His attachment for the Talented Tenth, however, waned. The Black intelligensia, particularly vulnerable to the economic sanctions readily imposed against Black social reformers, had, he felt, sold out. The Black educated elite emphasized the trappings of the White society and "integration" at the expense of their race. Instead of leading their race as he had envisioned, the middle-socioeconomic status Blacks had galvanized their resistance in opposition to those issues noxious to them as a middle class, and had failed to perform their messianic mission of elevating the mass of the Black workers. The Talented Tenth's value system soon reflected that of the middle-socioeconomic status Whites which they sought to emulate, and they had, in many ways, turned their backs on the Black communities from which they had "escaped."

In his 1930 address to the graduating class of Howard University, Du Bois stated that the fundamental paradox of Negro education still remained. The Black college had provided intelligent leadership but that leadership had not, as yet, comprehended the age in which it lived. The Black colleges and universities had had the proper liberal education method, but had fostered no goals. They had failed to recognize and deal with "the tremendous organization of industry, commerce, capital and credit which today forms a superorganization dominating and ruling the universe, subordinating to its ends government, democracy, religion, education and social philosophy . . ." (Du Bois 1973, p. 66).

A large proportion of Black college-trained students had entered the professions and sat perched on the periphery of White middle-socioeconomic status society, "depending for their support," Du Bois insisted, "upon an economic foundation which does not yet exist" (1973, p. 67). This position caused the Black "white collar proletariat" to live beyond their means possessing an "overwhelming appetite for wealth and no reasonable way of gratifying it, no philosophy for counteracting it" (Du Bois 1973, p. 67).

Negro industrial education had yielded pitifully small results, as the general economy was turning away from the agricultural, small business, and handcraftsmanship fields that were the specialties of Black industrial (or better, as John Hope Franklin claims) "vocational" education. Black vocational education, while guided by a definite object in view, failed because it lacked an appropriate method to attain that object. Vocational curricula emphasized farming, animal husbandry, carpentry, brick laying, plas-

tering, painting, and metal work in an era in which these trades were becoming automated out of existence. The real tragedy of the industrial school was that it had not evolved into the modern engineering and technological institution of the White community. The critical area of Black industrialism had fallen into the curriculum of neither the industrial school nor that of the college or university. Neither type of institution had addressed itself to the Black economic problems from the point of view of the Black worker. Neither had sought the development of Black trade unionism. Both had treated the laborer as the element to be molded to the will of management.

The time had arrived, Du Bois claimed, for the Black industrial school and the Black college to unite to produce graduates of broad vision, knowledge, and ideals, as well as persons proficient in the techniques of business, from the hand techniques through engineering and industrial planning. He called upon the race to ". . . establish a self-supporting organization to ensure its stability and our economic survival and eventual incorporation into world industry" (Du Bois 1973, p. 77).

He then concluded his Howard University address by stressing the ideals of poverty, work, knowledge, and sacrifice. Commenting on the Howard speech in a postscript, Du Bois stated:

The reception of this speech was kindly. I think it helped. But the speech lacked something. It was strong in exposition and criticism but weak in remedy. I was at this time in my social thought entering a wider and broader ocean, and I did not yet see clearly whither I was sailing. For that illumination, I have yet to wait. (1973, p. 82)

In the fall of 1940, Du Bois published his greatest work, *Dusk of Dawn: An Essay Toward an Autobiography of a Race Concept.* In that volume Du Bois reexamined the position of the Black race in America and charted a course for the future. He pointed out a path for Black men and women to follow with particular emphasis upon the long-neglected economic sphere. The social implications of the theory are clear, as are its pedagogical ramifications, for the person concerned about the education of Black youth and looking for alternatives to the time-worn extremes of integrationism and Black racism. Du Bois pointed to a third path leading toward "a culturally pluralistic society in which races were conserved and each race was in a position to make its unique contribution to society without any impediments" (Lester 1971, pp. 16-17).

It was at this particular juncture that Du Bois was to have a parting of the ways with the NAACP as his theory evolved along the collective economic action line as opposed to the legal action/integrationist philosophy of the NAACP.

The situation, as Du Bois perceived it, was such that:

It is impossible for the clear-headed student of human action in the United States and in the world, to avoid facing the fact of a white world which is today dominating human culture and working for the continued subordination of the colored races. (Du Bois 1968, p. 138)

The dominant White power brokers were convinced that the Black races had contributed nothing to the human evolution of culture. Du Bois particularly singled out educators in this condemnation.

I freely admit that, according to white writers, white teachers, white historians, *and white moulders of public opinion, nothing ever happened in the world of any importance that could not, or should not, be labeled "white."* [He continues, however,] *to be sure, good seed proves itself in the flower and the fruit, but the failure of seed to sprout is no proof that it is not good. It may be proof simply of the absence of manure—or its excessive presence. (Emphasis added.) (1968, p. 145)*

There is no "Negro Problem." There is an American problem, and that problem is White racism. The problems of Black people are the problems of poverty, of being "have-nots" in a society of "haves." The problem was not, and is not, the cultural deprivation of the Black race, because "race," itself, is, as Du Bois points out, a cultural fact. The problem was the Black race's lack of wealth, hence economic power, hence

political power in a plutocracy, a society in which power resides in the hands of the wealthy. Even the minority of the Black race who possessed wealth, the Talented Tenth, did so only with the permission of the dominating wealthy class. This tenuous grasp on wealth made that educated elite highly vulnerable to economic sanctions, thereby emasculating them. Until the Black race could generate an economic base to support a fiscally secure leadership, unfettered by White dominance, there could be no restructuring of the economic framework of America.

The caste system, the segregation of the Black race, was the incontrovertible fact of Black life in America. Black students attended separate schools; Black travelers rode on separate rail cars; Black patients were treated in separate health facilities; Black dead were laid to rest in separate cemeteries.

The potentially best course of action for the Black race was not to ignore the facts of this segregation, but to organize in order that they might control and improve those separate facilities. Du Bois says that he "came [to the 1933 Second Amenia Conference] advocating new deliberate and purposeful segregation for economic defense" (1968, p. 313). He says that this change in his emphasis was not a repudiation of the NAACP's efforts at desegregation, but that the integrationist path of the National Association would not work. It was a program without a goal that would recognize the unique Black cultural contribution.

The second path, that of the communists, ignored the obvious fact of the White race's hatred of the Black race. Its theory of social class conflict sought instead to unite the Black working people with the White workers, precisely that group that manifested the greatest hatred of the Black race. To Du Bois this alternative was nonsensical. Communism sought to restructure society through violence, based upon the premise that was the way in which the Soviet Union had accomplished its reorganization. They chose to ignore the various historical differences.

A reorganization of society was necessary, but Du Bois, the long-time pacifist, did not believe in the dogma of inevitable revolution. His third path advocated:

> . . . a project for a planned program of using the racial segregation which was at present inevitable, in order that the laboring masses might be able to have built beneath them a strong foundation for self-support and social uplift. (Du Bois 1968, p. 301)

Whereas previously they had focused upon the exceptional people, upon the Talented Tenth, upon the well-to-do, Black leaders must now turn their attention toward the welfare and social uplift of the Black masses. The Russian Revolution had set one admirable historical precedent. It had done one thing no other mass movement had previously done:

> It has made the assumption, long disputed, that out of the downtrodden masses of people, ability and character sufficient to do this task, could and would be found. I believed this dictum passionately. It was, in fact, the foundation stone of my fight for black folk; it explained me. (Du Bois 1968, p. 285)

By organizing the present victims of the caste system in a movement of mass social action, Du Bois's path would place "into the hands of those people who do the world's work the power to guide and rule the state for the welfare of the masses" (1968, p. 284). It would socialize the wealth of the Black community, organizing the acquisition of raw materials, the processing of those materials into finished goods, and the distribution of those goods and services in the best interest of the community. From this solid community economic base would come the funds necessary to develop jobs, houses, educational processes, health services, and transportation facilities necessary to deal with the problems peculiar to poverty: crime, high infant mortality rate, incidence of divorce, rate of illegitimacy.

He particularly advocated group education, organized and planned, so that those segregated schools would "become efficient, well-housed, well-equipped, with the best of teachers and with the best results on the children" (Du Bois 1968, p. 201). A good educational facility with well-trained and well-paid Black teachers was preferable to "forcing their children into white schools which met them with injustice and humiliation and discouraged their efforts to progress" (1968, p. 201).

The function of the schools was to prepare Black youths to take their place as productive members and leaders within the Black community to assist in its economic, social, political, and spiritual uplift. To do so the educational process must emphasize each individual's unique contribution to the community and his or her social responsibility to the community as a whole. It must emphasize the Black community's unique heritage and history as well as its particular contributions to the American social fabric. And it must recognize the unique position of the Black community as a model for the regeneration of American society. This model would be a democratic model in which power is not vested in the hands of a few but in the hands of many; a society which praises not the wealth of a few attained through the economic exploitation of many, but ensures the economic well-being of all.

This model could be used to rededicate the United States to the principle that governments are instituted among men to secure these inalienable rights of life, liberty, and the pursuit of happiness, and that governments derive their powers from the consent of the governed; and the democratic principle that the government which governs best reflects the expressed will of all of its citizens without regard to race, religion, ethnicity, or economic status; and the creative principle that states that in a multicultural society the government that promotes a forum for the expression of all of the myriad unique individual and cultural contributions of its citizenry affords itself the opportunity to consider a greater diversity of courses of action and is thereby better able to make progress in the areas of human freedom and social progress.

Du Bois did not envision the great liberal integrationist experiment of the 1960s, although he would certainly have applauded the tremendous inroads achieved by these struggles to desegregate many of the institutions and facilities in America. But the liberal experiment has ground to a halt. De jure segregation has been outlawed. But even a casual examination of the situation in the inner cities of the United States, both north and south, clearly indicates that either due to residence patterns or gerrymandering, the inner-city school is predominantly Black. Even a superficial analysis reveals that the problems of poverty persist. The fact that the violent resistance to forced busing has become a presidential campaign issue would seem to indicate that the transition into an integrated society is not smooth. The integrationist experiment has not alleviated the problem, because the problem is, as it was in 1940, White racism.

Any attempt to explain the situation solely in terms of socioeconomic status still ignores the equally important issue of race hatred. We have tried the integrationist path and, despite great successes, it has not ended the prejudice.

I agree with Du Bois that "no idea is perfect and forever valid. Always to be living and opposite and timely, it must be modified and adapted to changing facts" (1968, p. 303). So I do not recommend that we merely dredge up thirty-five-year-old ideas and offer them as a panacea for the three-hundred-year-old American problem of White racism. But I do feel that in the writings of W. E. B. Du Bois there is a culturally pluralistic alternative for the education of inner-city youth. This alternative proposes as a goal the education of Black youth to become leaders, leaders of a self-defining, self-directing Black community unfettered by White dominance. White professionals, teachers, doctors, attorneys, businesspeople, and social scientists are needed. They must teach and serve as leaders and models within the White community so that it might recognize and attempt to overcome the cancer of White racism that is destroying it from within. And White professionals are needed in the Black community, to assist in their respective fields until Black professionals are available.

But in the final analysis, the ultimate responsibility for the leadership, direction, and self-definition of the Black community must come from within. That leadership cannot exist on the support, and whim, of White philanthropy, but must draw its support economically, politically, socially, and psychologically, from a broad base within the Black community. Only when that leadership has firmly entrenched itself, can it, and those leaders of the White community committed to cultural pluralism, begin a systematic attempt to attach the twin cancers of racism and plutocracy that permeate our society. We are not celebrating the two-hundredth anniversary of the American Revolution. We are celebrating the two-hundredth year of the American revolutionary experiment for human rights and dignity in order that we might "secure the blessings of liberty to ourselves and our posterity."

References

Aptheker, H., ed. *The Education of Black People: Ten Critiques 1906-1960 by W. E. B. Du Bois.* Amherst, Mass.: University of Massachusetts Press, 1973.

Du Bois, W. E. B. *Dusk of Dawn: An Essay Toward an Autobiography of a Race Concept.* New York: Shocken Books, 1968.

Du Bois, W. E. B. Editorial in *Crisis,* June 1912. Quoted in *The Emerging Thought of W. E. B. Du Bois,* edited by H. L. Moon. New York: Simon & Schuster, 1972.

Du Bois, W. E. B. "Education and Work." In *The Education of Black People,* edited by H. Aptheker. Amherst, Mass.: University of Massachusetts Press, 1973.

Du Bois, W. E. B. *Souls of Black Folk.* New York: New American Library, 1969.

Franklin, J. H. *From Slavery to Freedom.* 3rd ed. New York: Alfred A. Knopf, 1967.

Hamilton, C. V. *The Black Experience in American Politics.* New York: G. P. Putnam's Sons, 1973.

Lester, J. *The Seventh Son: The Thought and Writings of W. E. B. Du Bois.* 2 vols. New York: Random House, 1971.

Moon, H. L., ed. *The Emerging Thought of W. E. B. Du Bois.* New York: Simon and Schuster, 1972.

Peeks, E. *The Long Struggle for Black Power.* New York: Charles Scribner's Sons, 1971.

Russell W. Irvine

The Explicit and Implicit Meaning of "Demythologizing the Inner-City Child"

Since 1950, books in the social and behavioral sciences, excluding anthropology, have used the term *myth*, or a kindred term such as *legend*, as part of the title more than twenty-five times.* During the decade of the 1950s, the term *myth* as part of book titles, was used only twice. During the 1960s, the term's popularity increased more than four times. In the half decade 1970 to 1975, the term appeared thirteen times or more than six times the rate over the decade of the 1950s.

Within the field of education, the inclination of authors to use the term *myth* shows a similar pattern of currency. For instance, in the half decade 1970 to 1975, educational writers employed, as part of their book titles, the term *myth* five times. No book titles which used the word *myth*

could be found for the decades of the 1950s or 1960s. Greer's *The Great School Legend* and Ginsburg's *The Myth of the Deprived Child* are examples of two recent works in the field of education which are perhaps best known.

Articles appearing in scholarly journals which make use of the term *myth* as part of the article title might be expected to further boost the popularity of the term by at least tenfold in each of the indicated decades. Underlying the use of this term, as with other ambiguous terms in printed material, appears to be the assumption made by authors that their readership will and does understand what is intended by the title designation and, secondly, that the title conveys apprehendable meaning to the reader. Indeed, the burden of responsibility for providing clarity and for defining terms rests with the author. Printed material, nevertheless, is a one-way communication process and, as such, interaction between the producer and the consumer is not implied.

However, in those instances where two-way communication is required or at least implied, such as in a conference setting, and where attention is called to terms only vaguely understood, such as in the title *Demythologizing the Inner-City Child*, the need for consensus on the definition of terms is imperative. Through analysis, this chapter attempts to rigorously define the terms used in designating this conference and, in the process, aid in specifying the general framework within which the success of the conference may be measured. What immediately follows is the rationale for this chapter, a general statement about the methodology used.

It might prove helpful to indicate why I have chosen to focus my attention on this conference title. My reason for choosing this approach may become clear as I attempt to indicate, in a limited way, some things about the nature of conference titles generally. To this end, let us assume a conference is to be held and the conference organizers have advertised for papers and symposia. In short, the appropriate audience is made aware of the conference. Individuals who wish to for-

---

*Data collected regarding the number of book titles carrying the term *myth* were obtained through perusal of the card catalogue at the Pullen Library of Georgia State University. No claim to an exhaustive bibliographic search is intended.

mally, or otherwise, participate in the conference are immediately presented with a problem involving precise interpretation of the intent of the conference by its title. The concern of this chapter is not with the attention-getting quality of conference titles but how individuals resolve the initial problem of understanding them.

Generally speaking, we may say that a conference title will be interpreted and understood in two ways. It may be taken in a manner suggestive of the conference content, intent, or objective. This interpretation of a conference title is perhaps the most common. On the other hand, its title may be interpreted in a literal sense, that is, taking the title at face value. A fairly strong case could be made that would justify the literal interpretation of a conference title. For example, it would seem legitimate to do so if the conference title is concrete and pointed and the potential contributors are clear as to the nature of the conference and their potential role in it.

It would seem legitimate, moreover, to do so if the terms in the conference title are in themselves provocative, that is, emotionally charged and/or subject to varying degrees of interpretation. Given that individuals are different and that the present contributors come from diverse backgrounds, there is a likelihood that there would not be consensus regarding the implied meaning of *Demythologizing the Inner-City Child.* Some form of analysis of the conference title is warranted, therefore, if any consensus is to be reached. Needless to say, however, consensus will not automatically be assured even under the most rigorous conditions of analysis. It is to the point of the provocative nature of the title in addition to the fact that it may be interpreted and understood in various ways, its intent notwithstanding, that is this conference's major source of weakness.

Each term in the conference title will be viewed as a separate component. After each term is viewed and its value weighed, I shall attempt to deal with the title as a total entity. Following this, I shall indicate what implication the title holds assuming a sociological posture.

DEMYTHOLOGIZING

The first word in the title to be considered is *demythologizing.* For the sake of convenience I shall omit the prefix and suffix of the word. The term under consideration, then, is *mythologize,* which relates to the process by which myths are either made, related, or constructed. To say that *mythologize* refers to the process by which myths are made or related begs the question: What is a myth? To answer this question we must state a few things about the evolutionary stage through which the term has passed. *Myth* in common usage is a borrowed term. The fields of anthropology and theology lay claim to the term's most "legitimate" and technical use. The transition from its former exclusive status in these fields has weakened the term and given it a more generic connotation. Therefore, the word *myth* is a nontechnical term lacking in clear meaning beyond the specific context in which it is used. It is in the manner of its popular use by social and behavioral scientists as well as by educators, parents, policymakers, and others that give the term *myth* its special but general social meaning.

Basic to the definition of a myth is the fact that they are "beliefs" that people hold. Designating a belief as a myth, however, suggests that such beliefs are in fact misbeliefs. A myth in this instance is more appropriately referred to as misunderstanding, misconceptualizing, or misapprehending some event, situation, or people. The term is usually reserved for those instances where a significant number of people share these misunderstandings or misconceptions. When referring to myths as suggested above, it may be useful to refer to them as "myths of the benign variety." Such an assignment helps to make the necessary distinction I believe ought to be made regarding the existence of a qualitative, different variety or form of myth which presents itself in American thought. Accordingly, we posit a second view of myths, a view in which myths assume a structure, a quality, and, psychologically speaking, a stereotype.

The two uses of the term may further be characterized in the following manner. A myth, understood in the first sense, assumes a more or less benign quality. It is much less psychologically entrenched and may be correctable, that is, subject to change in light of new knowledge or information which alters the misclassification or misunderstanding of events, objects, or people. Myths as stereotypes, on the other hand, are not easily subject to altering classification. In fact, such myths may be mildly or actively resistant to efforts to unseat them.

The two views of myths described above may be conceptually placed on a continuum. The distinguishing feature between them is their degree of intensity and effect when employed, as well as the respective extent to which each is alterable. In what sense may we understand the logical inference of *demythologizing?* Please note that the prefix of the term has been added.

Based upon this analysis, the term *demythologizing* should best be understood in the latter use of the term *myth,* since "benign myths" are relatively innocuous and characteristically alterable. To *demythologize,* meaning to reverse or negate various benign myths, would be a less substantive exercise and certainly not worthy of a formal conference. It is, therefore, concluded that *demythologizing* properly understood refers to the formidable task of attacking stereotypic attitudes and perceptions held, in this instance, about inner-city children.

INNER-CITY CHILD

We now turn our attention to the latter terms in the title, *inner-city child.* It should be stated that the term *inner city* has never been used by sociologists or educators with much precision. Such terms as *slum, ghetto,* and *poverty area,* among others, have all in their turn been used synonymously and interchangeably with *inner city.* It is beyond the scope of this chapter to undertake to rigorously define what an inner-city community is. It will suffice to point out some things inherent in the nature of communities generally.

When reference is made to the inner city, one usually has in mind either a geographical area with a characteristic ascribed as "low" status, or a combination of the physical characteristics of the area along with certain attendant psychological or pathological attributes of the inhabitants. The fact that such characterizations are overgeneralizations is beside the point; these mental images are what come to mind. An inner-city community, like all other types and forms of communities, is more or less politically, socially, and economically integrated. It may be studied with respect to this integration. Specifically, such things as how well it socializes or constrains the behavior of its members may be the focus of attention. The point to be made here is that an inner-city community is a status-independent area.

In contrast to the term *inner-city,* the concept of child or childhood is not status-independent. Childhood is rather a transitory period as well as a status-dependent period of life. Children can never be viewed as separate entities divorced from the social milieu of their parents. Any study or investigation into the phenomenon of childhood implicitly suggests a simultaneous inquiry into those factors which have produced and are producing the child, namely the significant adults in the child's environment. At the risk of splitting hairs, I venture the following observation regarding the terms *inner-city child.* The title combines a status-independent concept with a status-dependent concept. Let me hasten to add, however, that this concept incongruence evident in the title does not materially detract from its clarity. My point is that it is the entire inner-city complex which must be demythologized, not simply or exclusively its children. Myths, in other words, are not directly beamed at the children of these areas.

What, then, does the title *Demythologizing the Inner-City Child* mean sociologically? This question is neither simple nor can it be addressed frontally. Perhaps the best approach in hazarding an answer is to return to the pivotal term in the conference title, *mythologize.* The basic structure of this term, as we have explained, is that it is the process of relating or imposing myths. Underlying this process is the ability or power to have myths imposed upon a group independent of their will. Two new elements are introduced by this process. It suggests that some form of group interaction is involved and that these groups share differential power resources in relationship to each other. As indicated above, the fact that "lower" status communities with distinct population groupings can be compared and contrasted to "higher" status communities with distinct populations further supports the implied notion that social power factors are operating. To the extent that "negative" myths about inner-city children exist, such myths are functional fabrications of power-holding groups outside these communities. In a manner of speaking, myths are psychological tools of domination. More accurately stated, myths are by-products of these power relationships.

Caution is called for lest the impression is conveyed that myths are more tangible than might be supposed. The opposite impression is closer to the reality of their nature. This analysis reveals, in addition to the feature of myths stated above, that myths are an abstract mental orientation, perhaps dispositions which are lodged in the belief system of a group. These belief systems organize, to a greater or lesser extent, the manner in which problems are approached, objects are classified, people are categorized and reacted to, and so forth. More generally put, it frames their world view. To seriously examine the myths surrounding the inner-city child or, for that matter, myths about the dominating group itself, provides a glimpse into the organization of that world view. To use different words, one sees how the "they" and "we" groups in a society are valued.

MYTH IMPOSITION

A more complete answer to our question (What does the title *Demythologizing the Inner-City Child* mean sociologically?) can be found if we understand the broader ideological under-

pinning of the American society. While time and space preclude any detailed analysis of context, a few observations about it should serve to make the point. As has been suggested, the imposition of various myths upon inner-city people is fundamentally a function of a differential power relationship. There is a suggestion, which I do not want to convey, in asserting that myth impositions are always a conscious act or some conspiratorial plot by the ruling power groups to render the subordinate group more powerless. Some benefit is derived by the power-holding group when myths have this effect, however. A more accurate assessment of what is involved here is revealed by C. Wright Mills (1959, Chapter 13). Mills attempts to make the distinction between what characterizes an autonomous public of informed and opinion formulating people and an opinion monopolized mass of people. The former he terms a "society of the publics" and the latter a "society of the masses." Though neither pure type of society empirically exists, Mills argues that America is drifting in the direction of the latter type of society. In characterizing the "society of the masses," Mills suggests that mass media, both the visual and the printed forms, have had the greatest impact upon what we think, how we think, how we ought to behave, what we should wear, and so forth. In short, mass media, including education, have monopolized and penetrated every sphere of public life.

Mills outlines four characteristics which have had the greatest influence in the "public" to "mass" transformation. The first characteristic relates to the information dispensing apparatus of mass communication, more specifically the "rate of the givers of opinion to the receivers." Two ideal forms of communication are identified. At one extreme is a one-to-one communication process, that is, two people involved in mutual and personal expressions of ideas and views. At the other extreme is a one-to-multimillion type relationship. Here one individual via mass communication technology is able to dispense information, ideas, views, opinions, and values to an infinite number of people. In the former type mutuality and personality involvement is inherently suggested. In the latter type, however, no such mutuality is suggested nor may be possible.

The second characteristic is a corollary of the first and has to do with "the possibility of answering back an opinion." The technology of mass communication, while not technically excluding such a possibility, obviates it in the main. The monopolistic interests of mass media decide who shall answer back an opinion, when, and for how long. Such controls, when exercised, produce asymmetry in the formulation and the dissemination of information.

The third characteristic relates to the consequences for social action under conditions where characteristics one and two are fully realized. Broadly speaking, collective action is precluded to the extent that necessary information bearing on such action is available. Information and articulated opinions are necessary preconditions for social action.

The final characteristic centers attention on the extent to which the public is free, that is, autonomous and independent of institutional authority. Important to this dimension is the degree to which authority controls and sanctions the individuals whose actions are guided by public discussions. Under conditions where total control is exercised by institutional authorities, the influence of public debate as guides to action is nullified.

The implication of control of the channels of communication, essentially forestalling various forms of public discussion and debate, are far-reaching in significance. It is maintained here that since the autonomous character of American life is rapidly being eroded, myths function as substitutes for serious public debate and discussion. Myths thrive in environments devoid of substantive opportunity for serious and searching inquiry. The control of the public through the monopoly of mass media not only victimizes the "general" population but also those on whom the "general" population prey, namely, the powerless of the inner city.

Reference

Mills, C. W. "The Mass Society." *The Power Elite*. New York: Oxford University Press, 1959.

Asa G. Hilliard

The Education of "Inner-City" Children

Teachers in a deep sense are the makers of individual personality and character, and hence of culture, society or civilization. Teachers are the mediators of such truth and the chief advocates of a continuous search for truth. If they no longer believe the search has meaning, the whole process becomes a hoax and a sham. (Pullias 1975, p. 1)

Herein, however, lies no argument for the oft-heard contention that education for the white man should mean one thing and for the Negro a different thing. The element of race does not enter here. It is merely a matter of exercising common sense in approaching people through their environment in order to deal with conditions as they are rather than as you would like to see them or imagine that they are. (Woodson 1933, p. xxxi)

A few weeks ago I had a second chance to see Lenore Wiesman's slide tape show on sex-role stereotyping in children's literature. In a very powerful way, this presentation demonstrated the way in which messages are sent to children through seemingly innocent educational materials. There is no doubt about it, the racism and sexism of our larger society are reflected in professional materials. However, in this second viewing of the tapes, I was struck even more by the fact that the overwhelming majority of the pictures which were evaluated for the film were *illustrations* of reality and not *photographs!* It occurred to me that the matter of stereotyping in these pictures could be resolved very quickly simply by changing the illustrations. However, that by itself would not be likely to change the real world. Not only that, but changes could be made toward more equity in our picture images of reality and at no point after that would we and our children be compelled to look at the real world.

Why are there so few photographs in children's literature of things as they really are? Is it a matter of cost? Are photographs less interesting? My interest was piqued even more because I was mindful of the theme of the conference, *Demythologizing the Inner-City Child.* I had become highly sensitized to the prevalence of a general disposition in our profession to make plans and decisions based upon *images* and *abstractions* rather than upon reality. As I reviewed the primary sources of information for children and adults, I saw that the situation in children's literature is only a part of a larger pattern. Increasingly we have come to rely upon television and films to provide experience in place of our own direct observation and participation. The big sellers seem to be *dramatizations* which are closer to fantasy than to reality. As I review much of our professional practice and scholarship, I find that this *malady of abstraction and myth* is endemic. Analogous to the illustrations in children's literature is much of our professional jargon and our so-called research which comes from trying to see people through paper rather than in more direct ways.

Children's literature seldom carries powerful morals any more. But this is also true of television, movies, and our professional and scholarly work. We rely upon manufactured excitement and thrills to keep our interest. I cannot help but feel that we are in danger of becoming addicted to myth, fantasy, and amorality. If this is true, then we have the context which explains the emergence of what I believe to be the *myth of the "inner-city" child*. Take a closer look with me at what we call the "inner-city" child and at how we come to know that child.

For many years, I have been appalled at the damage done to Afro-American children in the name of help and scholarship. It often seems that years of professional "help" and "quality" scholarship have resulted in little gain and most often in losses for children. Educators seldom point with pride of accomplishment to the education of children in large urban areas. What is the justification for continuing to sink money into such things as massive testing and developmental screening programs when there is no clear connection between the use of these tools and gains for children? Why should so many highly trained "specialists" be assigned to urban schools when the results of this work may often be little more than professional explanations for the children's lack of progress? Why continue to fund research studies and evaluations on children and schools when those who do these studies never seem to provide the keys to success in working with children in urban areas? On the other hand, why is the visibility so low for the many models of success? I was delighted to hear the Governor of Georgia announce that one of his priorities is education and that he wants recommendations on *things that work*. I believe that the time is here for each one of us to say clearly what we believe we can accomplish, and for each of us to remain in the struggle to improve education for children *only* if we can deliver success.

For a period of time in education and other helping professions, it seemed, by some of the more inventive names we used to label school experiences, that we truly and fully understood learning and teaching dynamics and that we had solutions to our problems of how to influence

child growth. You know the following terms: "dyslexia," "Head Start," "minimal brain dysfunction," "sociogenic brain damage," "culturally deprived," "restricted language code," "broken home," "single parent families," "readiness," "educationally handicapped," "multicultural," and "inner city." They all carried either an implied diagnosis or treatment. Certainly these activities and labels, in many if not most cases, have really represented a silent assault on millions of Black, Brown, and poor children. As we think today of child abuse, we must not exclude these acts of labeling, for they are often more gross and insidious than overt physical acts of abuse, because they cripple the minds and spirits of families, children, and professional practitioners alike. The abuse is even more gross and insidious when we note that the mythology about children and professional practice often continues even in the face of hard evidence to the contrary. In short, we do not know some of the things which we claim to know, and we ought to know some things which we seem not to know . . . but more about that later.

Usually, when we say "inner-city" we simply use it as a euphemism for Black, Brown, or other poor children. I have come to feel that there is no way to deal with the task of demythologizing these Afro-American, Mexican-American, or poor children unless we turn a sharp diagnostic and prescriptive eye to both the myths and the mythmakers. An effective attack on this problem requires some guesses about the origin of the myths. Why do mythmakers make myths? We will take a closer look at the myths and the mythmakers. First, however, I want to make some observations about the importance of the analysis of myth in professional practice.

THE PROFESSIONAL CONDITION

The field of education practice is still in its infancy. We do not yet have much in the way of a clearly defined and agreed upon body of valid knowledge and professional skills; that is, a knowledge of skills which, if properly applied, will guarantee that children will learn better than they would if the teacher did not possess such knowledge and skills. The knowledge and skill base will come in time.

In the meantime, however, we are painfully aware of our mission at conscious and unconscious levels. We are sometimes fearful of being found wanting. We may not feel potent, especially where the task is to educate Afro-American, Mexican-American, and poor children. The mounting failure rates of these children, in urban areas in particular, continually confront us as a bad dream which is fast becoming a nightmare. We may not know where to turn and cannot confront the impotence which we manifest. There is too much at stake. We have invested too many years, dollars, hopes, and too much "face" in becoming teachers. We have done all that was asked of us and all that we know to do. There are no other jobs for many of us. Most of us want to be successful. In this condition we need—no, we demand—a belief system which will make everything seem all right, even if that means a retreat to the world of myth. We do not have to create myths. However, we become ripe for the charlatan with quack cures or for the spinner of professional yarns, the mythmaker. But as with all narcotics, the myth fails us in the long run, and it takes larger and larger doses just to stay even. With all its problems, the real pro demands the real world.

There is now a general belief system about education which includes things pertaining to the education of Afro-American, Mexican-American, and poor children. This belief system is the product of our history and is fed constantly by a stream of contemporary myths. This belief system is situated in our social-cultural context in 1976. It can be understood only by reference to the historical antecedents of our nation. These antecedents include, but are not limited to, such things as colonialism, slavery, racism, genocide, a North American population explosion, rapid industrialization, technological success, military power, wealth, and an increasing seculari-

zation. Out of the cataclysmic three hundred to four hundred year period of recent history, we have come to believe certain things about ourselves, others, and the world, which govern the way we think and act. We have almost no systematically developed information about what these things are or how they affect our beliefs and practice in education, and more specifically the education of Afro-American, Mexican-American, and poor children. For example, our past affects our answers to such questions as: Do Afro-American, Mexican-American, and poor children have the capacity to learn? Can children be "educated" in racially segregated schools? It is in this context that questions about the education of children have meaning.

While many of us have some knowledge of the history just mentioned, few of us will have understood how that history has shaped professional belief and behavior. For example, it took a special kind of scholarship and educational practice to help achieve a climate and train a citizenry that would foster and perpetuate slavery and racism. Sociology, anthropology, psychology, etc., were pressed into service to deliver information clothed in the trappings of science—to make things *seem* right (Kamin 1974; Montague 1974; Lewis 1973; Rodney 1974; Thomas and Sillen 1972; Woodward 1966; Valentine and Valentine 1975).

Right on schedule our scholarly forefathers brought forth on this continent a new belief system about the world's people. Color and intelligence were suddenly correlated where they had not been so in history before. Scholars have had assistance. The libraries of the Ethiopians, Nubians, Egyptians, West Africans at Timbuctoo, the Hebrew Toldoth, the Library of the Mayans, and the records of Afro-Americans during the United States reconstruction were *destroyed*, suppressed, or ignored so that some highly respected scholars could say that only Europeans had a real history (Du Bois 1973; Forbes 1973; James 1954; Mead 1968; Williams 1974).

Some scholars also have been frantic to prove the genetic inferiority of the people of color for many years now (Thomas and Sillen 1972). Comparative studies of cranial capacity, cerebral contuberances, and egocentric and ethnocentrically developed "IQ" tests were the vehicles. Even today massive grants are given to carry this work on at a more sophisticated level. Studies of genetics for the purpose of discovery or prediction in the uterus or at least in childhood of "potential or predelinquents" or "potential or precriminality" are often the new code labels for an old racist quest. Many of these will become the ridiculous documents of tomorrow, just as many of the professional fathers look ridiculous today when their works are read in the original. It is not their scientific opinions which we ridicule; it is their opinions without even the pretense of science which they tried to sell as the real thing that make them pathetic figures (Hilliard 1975a; Kamin 1974; Thomas and Sillen 1972).

The legacy of that pathos is still with us, and yet I look in vain for serious study of these matters in our "foundations of education" courses at the university. Could it be that we in the universities are not knowledgeable about the true foundations of our educational discipline? Is racism in scholarship a matter of no significance for our understanding of research and professional practice? Can a teacher or professor be said to be *qualified* who has no understanding of this major variable in our professional lives? Is our teacher education curriculum complete?

COMMON MYTHS THAT EDUCATORS LIVE BY

. . . we are just completing five years of intimate involvement as anthropologists in an inner-city Afro-American community, one of the principal types of community to which concepts like "sociogenic brain damage" are meant to apply. This research experience has given us an increasingly deep sense of skepticism toward learned portrayals and analyses of oppressed social groupings in the United States. This essay is thus part of a long-term effort to understand how and why direct experience of Afro-American life is so radically at odds with the constructions continually emerging from the social sciences and related fields of scholarly and specialized study. . . . We are convinced that in general these issues have been wrongly con-

ceived, spuriously argued, and falsely presented to a public all too ready to misperceive them. (Valentine and Valentine 1975, p. 117)

I leave you with these questions and turn now to a slightly more detailed articulation of myths from the common core of the contemporary belief system of our profession. I regard these myths as symptoms of a broadly-based professional distemper. Here are a few which I believe are widely accepted either explicitly or by implication from our general professional practice.

1. We tend to believe that *poverty environments are cognitively deprived* (Bernstein 1960; Jensen 1969).

2. We tend to believe that *racism is not a variable in teaching and learning.* Virtually no studies of teaching and learning attempt even in gross fashion to conceptualize, assess, and control for racism.

3. We tend to believe that *knowledge of IQ scores leads to effective instructional strategies.* In a ritualized fashion, millions of dollars are spent to get scores which have never been shown to provide data that is related to learning gains.

4. We tend to believe that *language which adults hear children using or language which teachers hear Black children using is the only language that those children have.* Millions of Afro-American, Mexican-American, and poor children are denied the use in education of their rich, complex, culturally-situated language and experiences.

5. We tend to believe that *learning is language dependent, especially White common English.* Even animals learn without specific human words, why not children?

6. We tend to believe that *children can be studied without being affected by those who study them.* In many of the research studies today, researchers' reports are limited to scores or they are reports about *child* behavior without any data concerning researcher involvement in the child's world.

7. We tend to believe that *high level reasoning is beyond the reach of children.* Any appreciation of the mental operations which are required for language acquisition would show this to be false (Hilliard 1975b).

8. We tend to believe that *we know the components of and sequences for learning to read and to handle quantities.* We are just beginning. We will learn that there are an unlimited number of ways to learn, not a single one (Ramiréz and Castañeda 1974).

9. We tend to believe that *children believe what we say more than what we do or feel.* If we did not believe this, a greater proportion of our teacher education time would be spent in an examination of how messages are sent and how to use these channels rather than with a "logical" arrangement of content.

10. We tend to believe that *children have no agenda of their own.* In fact, standardized tests, curriculum, teaching, etc., cannot work for the very reason that children do have agendas, priorities, and goals of their own. Skilled teachers are able to find out what these are and use them in teaching.

11. We tend to believe that *professional diagnostic categories in education generally refer to real observable behaviors.* Many of the popular labels which we use have no basis in reality (Schrag and Divoky 1975; Kamin 1974; Senna 1973).

12. We tend to believe that *there is one standard model which describes all children.* There is no one model child. There are many different "inner-city" children as well.

CHARACTERISTICS OF MYTHMAKERS

These are some of the myths which hurt the Afro-American, Mexican-American, and poor children in particular. What keeps these myths going? What are the mythmakers like? Recognition is half of the battle to protect our children. It is particularly important in the developing field of education, with its vulnerability to mythology, that we develop frameworks for assessing truth and reality. I find that mythmakers are fairly easy to describe. Their behavior is clearly visible to the prepared observer.

1. *Mythmakers rely upon jargon or "word salad."* Their labels have no valid experiential referents. The label "minimal brain dysfunction" is a prime example (Schrag and Divoky 1975); it has an enormous list of fuzzy symptoms which are often contradictory. "IQ" is another; there is no common meaning from one test to another, nor do users share a common definition.

2. *Mythmakers establish perceptual distance between themselves and the children whom they purport to know.* They are seldom identified with the children nor can their experience with the populations which are studied be said to be intimate.

3. *Mythmakers highlight discussions of process in teaching but seldom demonstrate that the process described is tied to child gains.* New things for teachers to do are taught to teachers (competency-based teacher education). However, there is seldom a guarantee that a teacher who masters the selected competencies will be able to produce student gains or that anyone else has ever produced student gains as a consequence of using the competencies.

4. *Mythmakers usually are most intimately familiar with paper (journal articles, reports, statistical procedures) and seldom with adults and almost never with children, particularly Afro-American, Mexican-American, or poor children.*

5. *Mythmakers tend to study Afro-American, Mexican-American, and poor children and their families in isolation from the range of things that affect these children and their families.* Typical of this principle is the fact that research on Afro-American, Mexican-American, and poor children seldom if ever includes information about the background of the researcher in any systematic way. Yet, as an observer, *the researcher is an experimental variable* as he or she interferes with children's responses by intrusion and by imposing an often alien frame of reference in interpreting data.

6. *Mythmakers are frequently personally, professionally, and economically invested in their myths.* For example, the profession of psychology seems unable to rise against the abusive IQ tests largely because many psychologists feel that they would have nothing else professionally to offer if they had no IQ tests to administer and to interpret. Pathetic! But in many cases, this is exactly the case when the psychologist studies people who are different from himself or herself.

7. *Mythmakers tend to rely upon jargon and especially professional gadgetry for professional credibility rather than highlighting their successful relationships with children.*

8. *Mythmakers tend toward a selective use of data.* There is a peculiar myopia regarding success in education. For example, to my knowledge no major professional journal has carried a study or analysis of the most outstanding example of teaching I have yet to witness. Project Special Elementary Education for the Disadvantaged (SEED) is 12 years old and has never failed to teach Afro-American, Mexican-American, poor, and foreign populations of children to do college level math at grades from kindergarten through sixth grade. This dramatic demonstration shatters the Jensen Hypothesis about genetics and IQ (note that Jensen's Hypothesis comes from his study of paper, not from his clinical skill). Without any apologies for "low IQ," "perceptual deficits," "nutritional deficits," "broken homes," "cultural deprivation," "restricted language codes," or "low self-concept," William Johntz, a White male, and the hundreds of teachers he has trained get astounding results! To see Afro-American and other children multiplying two four-digit numbers in their heads, doing logarithms and exponents and begging for more makes some researchers liars and other researchers incompetents.

Why are there no professionals rushing to find out why these children all over the nation do so well? Why when this all began in Jensen's own city of Berkeley does he seem unaware that his predictions do not work, and why does he con-tinue to plod through the reams of paper? Why does he still draw so much professional attention when Johntz and his workers remain virtually unknown?

9. *Mythmakers are unable to detect absurdities.* For example, the mythmakers in the IQ and genetics controversy have taken no note of the extreme differences in the proportion of Black male to Black females in classes designated for the mentally retarded. Another undetected absurdity is to study the child only, in order to diagnose problems, instead of studying all environmental main effects simultaneously.

10. *Mythmakers always have a narrow focus.* They do not call upon sociocultural data and historical perspectives. They are time-bound, culture-bound, and are oblivious to their condition.

THE BACKGROUND FOR PROFESSIONAL CHANGE

Unfortunately, [much of the research in education is done in such a way that it obscures information about highly successful teaching and sensitive, competent research.] These examples are lost in a sea of statistical averages. Sophisticated investigators from many ethnic backgrounds have produced verifiable reports of children's behavior which shows that all ethnic groups function on about the same mental plane when solving problems using their own environmental data (Cole and Scribner 1974; Evans 1970; Ginsburg 1972; Kamin 1974; Ainsworth 1973). I find it pitiful indeed that most of these works and other scholarly works, which are relevant in a fundamental way to professional practice with the so-called inner-city child, are virtually absent from the syllabi, reference lists, library reserve lists, and bookstore shelves where teachers are educated. And yet few students of education and psychology today are spared the work of A. R. Jensen. The simple report of Jay (1971) on the background of Afro-Americans who hold a doctorate in natural science shows that certain Afro-American high schools and Black undergraduate colleges were consistently successful in producing graduates who could more than hold their own at the finest universities. Yet our professional education programs today in Black or White institutions seldom have the data for speculation or research on the causes of that success. However, we do have as common content the work of Jencks and Coleman who suggest that school factors have minimal effects on pupil success.

The doctrines of such thinkers as Dewey, Illich, Plato, Gieger, and others are usually considered as basic to the education of teachers, even though none of these thinkers are known for their understanding of the urban multiethnic milieu and problems. As might be expected the profound, gritty, and relevant work of Woodson (1933), as well as that of Du Bois (1973) and Forbes (1973), are uniformly overlooked. Our historical perspectives in education are based upon the standard names such as R. Freeman, Butts, and others, yet the work of scholars such as Bullock (1967) is unknown. Under such circumstances, how can there be anything other than myths about Afro-Americans, Mexican-Americans, Asian-Americans, and therefore Euro-Americans? Euro-American history and pedagogy, then, must be seen as counterfeit to the extent that it cannot be accurate if it fails to take into account an accurate history and pedagogy of all other Americans, for they are all inextricably intertwined.

Not only is there basic foundations content currently available and immediately applicable and useful for better teacher education, but there is an emerging pedagogy which is valid as well. The myth of teaching as a mystical process has already been put to rest by Johntz in Project SEED* and, more recently, by the work of Tikunoff, Berliner, and Rist (1975) in California.

In the case of Johntz, teaching practice is based upon two fundamental principles. *First, the teacher of a subject must know that subject in*

Project SEED is now a federally funded project which has its headquarters in Berkeley, CA, at the Lawrence Hall of Science.

depth. Second, the teacher uses the responses of the children to build instructional strategies on the spot. A kind of on-going "miscue analysis" and questioning is done. SEED teachers know that most children respond to the questions that they "hear" and with the assumptions that they hold. Teaching, then, is a matter of learning, as a teacher, precisely what question a student is answering and what assumptions that student holds. Then, by skillful questioning, both the question and the assumptions are changed to assist a child in expanding his or her responses to include new questions and assumptions. This is done without gimmicks, mediated packages, small classes, or other help. Only a piece of chalk and a blackboard are used. The training process for a SEED teacher is a continuing, peer feedback, open, rigorous, collaborative, and carefully designed process. Through their own self-evaluation, SEED teachers have identified well over a hundred specific strategies which they use to accomplish remarkable results.

The work at the Far West Regional Laboratory dovetails beautifully with some of the pedagogy utilized in Project SEED. Researchers at the Laboratory have used one group of classrooms where student achievement was very high and another group where student achievement was very low. Lessons were taught for the same period of time toward the same objectives. Using student achievement gains as the criterion for successful teaching, ethnographers were assigned to each classroom. These ethnographers developed detailed observation data (protocols) which were then analyzed by other raters.

From this very involved study, 61 dimensions were identified which separated the teachers in the high-achieving classrooms from those in the low-achieving classrooms. In one of the rare studies in professional literature, we find that there are teacher behaviors which are associated with student success. Interestingly enough, the dimensions of teacher behavior include many which good teacher educators have known about for some time. The high-achieving teachers were described in part as follows:

Instructional Moves

More attending	More open questions
Less abruptness	More pacing
More drilling	More praising
More encouraging	Less rushing
More equity	More spontaneity
More ethnicity	Less stereotyping
Less filling time	More structuring
Fewer illogical statements	More teacher-made
More mobility	materials
More monitoring	Less time fixedness
of learning	More waiting

Teacher Behavior Control Moves

Less belittling	Less moralizing
More consistency	Less policing
of message	More personalizing
Less excluding	Less sarcasm
Less Less harassing	Less shaming
Less ignoring	More signaling
More modeling	

Teacher Characteristics

More accepting	More job satisfaction
More awareness of	More knowledge
developmental level	of subject
Less trying to be liked	More optimism
More defending	More warmth

Here we have, in two unusual studies, clear student gains with similar explanations for success. Not in either case is there a study of the students, their families, their IQ, or other factors. The message seems clear. The fastest and surest way to demythologize Afro-American, Mexican-American, poor, or other "inner-city" children is to demythologize the teaching process by highlighting successful practice and by articulating *that* practice. Such an approach would relegate to the research laboratory much of what now consumes so much of our time. Why continue to pretend that IQ testing helps in teaching? Why continue to pretend that knowledge about popular pseudoarguments among unsuccessful but famous and respected researchers is a prerequisite to successful teaching? Why should we make life miserable for ourselves and our children by becoming continuously absorbed in the literature of deficit and ex-cuse making? If we must have a guru, why pick the one who has no track record, who has never solved problems? Why not make those who speak through paper (journals, books, equations, etc.) show us what they mean in practice? Why use professional language or jargon when we do not know what it means or if it has no utility?

This is 1976. A new declaration of independence is in order. We must declare our independence from invalid scholarship, from high priests of academia (unless "money and mouth" are together), and from the hopelessness and despair that makes working in our cities' poverty pockets seem so impossible. No, we cannot solve all the problems which have been created by an uncaring and often hostile society. But a little good teaching can go a long way. Our problem, then, will be what to do with the child awakened. Can we handle it when all those children do read, write, and compute? For they too will declare their independence, and where do we stand on that? The so-called inner-city child is alive and well. Are we? Will we be?

Now the great fear has been variously named and designated. It has been called in the past, Mob-rule, Sans-Cullotism, the Yellow Peril, the Negro Problem, and Social Equality. Whatever it is called, the foundation of the great fear is this: When a human being becomes suddenly conscious of the tremendous powers lying latent within him, when from the puzzled contemplation of a half-known self, he rises to the powerful assertion of a self, conscious of its might, then there is loosed upon the world possibilities of good or of evil that make men pause. And when this happens in the case of a class or nation or a race, the world fears or rejoices according to the way in which it has been trained to contemplate a change in the conditions of the class or race in question. . . . [Du Bois (1906) 1973, p. 8]

References

Ainsworth, M.D. "Sensorimotor Development of Ganda Infants." In *The Competent Infant: Research and Commentary*, edited by L. J. Stone, H. T. Smith, and L. B. Murphy. New York: Basic Books, 1973.

Beckum, L. C. *School Desegregation and Cultural Pluralism*. San Francisco: Far West Laboratory for

Educational Research and Development, 1975.

Bernstein, B. "Language and Social Class." *British Journal of Sociology* 2 (1960): 271-276.

Bullock, H. A. *A History of Negro Education in the South from 1619 to Present.* New York: Praeger, 1967.

Charnofsky, S. *Educating the Powerless.* Belmont, Calif.: Wadsworth Publishing Co., 1971.

Cole, M., and Scribner, S. *Culture and Thought: A Psychological Introduction.* New York: John Wiley & Sons, 1974.

Du Bois, W. E. B. *Black Reconstruction in America.* New York: Atheneum, 1973. (Originally published in 1935.)

Du Bois, W. E. B. *The Education of Black People.* New York: Monthly Review Press, 1973.

Evans, J. L. *Children in Africa: A Review of Psychological Research.* New York: Teachers College Press, 1970.

Forbes, J. D. *Aztecas Del Norte: The Chicanos of Aztlan.* Greenwich, Conn.: Fawcett, 1973.

Forbes, J. D. *Native Americans of California and Nevada.* Healdsburg, Calif. Naturegraph, 1969.

Ginsburg, H. *The Myth of the Deprived Child: Poor Children's Intellect and Education.* Englewood Cliffs, N.J.: Prentice-Hall, 1972.

Hilliard, A. G. "Science Under Colonialism and Racism: Impact on the Mind and Behavior," submitted for publication, 1975a.

Hilliard, A. G. "The Strengths and Weaknesses of Cognitive Tests for Young Children." In *One Child Indivisible,* edited by J. D. Andrews, pp. 17-33. Washington, D.C.: National Association for the Education of Young Children, 1975b.

James, G. G. M. "Stolen Legacy," unpublished manuscript, 1954.

Jay, J. M. *Negroes in Science: Natural Science Doctorates, 1876 to 1969.* Detroit: Ballap Publishing, 1971.

Kamin, L. *The Science and Politics of IQ.* New York: Halsted Press, 1974.

Jensen, A. R. "How Much Can We Boost IQ and Scholastic Achievement." *Harvard Educational Review* 39 (1969): 1-123.

King, L. L. *Confessions of a White Racist.* New York: Viking Press, 1969.

King, L. M. *African Philosophy: Assumptions and Paradigms for Research on Black Persons.* Los Angeles: Fanon Research & Development Center, 1975.

Lewis, D. "Anthropology and Colonialism." *Current Anthropology* 14 (December 1973): 581-602.

Levi-Strauss, C. *The Savage Mind.* Chicago: University of Chicago Press, 1962.

Mandler, J., and Stein, G. "The Myth of Perceptual Deficit." San Diego, Calif.: University of California, San Diego, 1975.

Mead, G. R. S. *Did Jesus Live 100 B.C.: An Inquiry in the Talmud Jesus Stories, Toldoth Jeschu, and Some Curious Statements of Epiphanius—Being a Contribution to the Study of Christian Origins.* New Hyde Park, New York: University Books, 1968. (Originally published in 1903.)

Montagu, A. *Man's Most Dangerous Myth: The Fallacy of Race.* New York: Oxford University Press, 1974. (Originally published in 1942.)

Montagu, A., ed. *The Concept of Race.* New York: Collier, 1964.

Nimnicht, G. P.; Johnson, J. A., Jr.; et al. *Beyond "Compensatory Education": A New Approach to Educating Children.* San Francisco: Far West Laboratory for Research and Development, 1973.

Nobles, W. W. "Psychological Research and the Black Self-Concept: A Critical Review." *Journal of Social Issues* 29 (1973): 11-30.

Pierce, C. M. "Psychiatric Problems of the Black Minority." In *American Handbook of Psychiatry: Child and Adolescent Psychiatry, Socio-cultural and Community Psychiatry,* Vol. II, edited by S. Arieti, pp. 512-523. New York: Basic Books, 1974.

Pullias, E. V. *A Common Sense Philosophy for Modern Man: A Search for Fundamentals.* New York: Philosophical Library, 1975.

Ramiréz, M., III, and Castañdea, A. *Cultural Democracy, Bicognitive Development, and Education.* New York: Academic Press, 1974.

Rodney, W. *How Europe Underdeveloped Africa.* Washington, D.C.: Howard University Press, 1974.

Rogers, J. A. *Nature Knows No Color-Line: Research into the Negro Ancestry in the White Race.* New York: Helga M. Rogers, 1952.

Sandmeyer, B. C. *The Anti-Chinese Movement in California.* Chicago: University of Chicago Press, 1973.

Schrag, P., and Divoky, D. *The Myth of the Hyperactive Child and Other Means of Child Control.* New York: Pantheon Books, 1975.

Senna, C., ed. *The Fallacy of IQ.* New York: Third Press, 1973.

Silberman, M. L. *The Experience of Schooling.* New York: Holt, Rinehart and Winston, 1971.

Smith, B. O.; Cohen, S. B.; and Pearl, A. *Teachers for the Real World.* Washington, D.C.: American

Association of Colleges for Teacher Education, 1969.

Smith, G., and Kniker, C. R. *Myth and Reality: A Reader in Educational Foundations.* Boston: Allyn and Bacon, 1972.

Thomas, A., and Sillen, S. *Racism and Psychiatry.* New York: Brunner/Mazel, 1972.

Tikunoff, W. J.; Berliner, D.C.; and Rist, R. C. *Special Study A: An Ethnographic Study of the Forty Classrooms of the Beginning Teacher Evaluation Study Known Sample.* San Francisco: Far West Laboratory for Educational Research and Development, Technical Report No. 75-10-5, 1975.

Valentine, C. A., and Valentine, B. A. "Brain Damage and the Intellectual Defense of Inequality." *Current Anthropology* 16 (1975): 117-150.

Williams, C. *The Destruction of Black Civilization: Great Issues of a Race from 4500 B.C. to 2000 A.D.* Chicago: Third World Press, 1974.

Whorf, B. L. *Language, Thought and Reality.* Cambridge, Mass.: M.I.T. Press, 1956.

Woodson, C. G. *The Mis-education of the Negro.* Washington, D.C.: Associated Publishers, 1933.

Woodward, C. V. *The Strange Career of Jim Crow.* New York: Oxford University Press, 1966. (Originally published in 1955.)

Intelligence
and Testing

Intelligence and testing are perhaps the most emotionally charged topics related to the psychology and education of inner-city children. It seems that nearly all professional and lay persons hold strong positions on such specific issues as the heritability of intelligence and the cultural bias of tests.

In an expository chapter drawing upon his own and other persons' research, Leonard Jacobson examines in detail three time-worn yet powerful myths. These are the myths that science has demonstrated unequivocally that the peoples of the earth can be reliably and validly classified according to the merit of their genetic potential, that we now understand the relationships between genetics and complex human behavior, and that intelligence has been adequately defined. Jacobson clearly illustrates the lack of empirical support for each of these myths and further illustrates the leaps of faith necessary for adhering to them.

If intelligence itself is not the most controversial area addressed in this book, then certainly testing is. Joanne Nurss has just completed a revision of the Metropolitan Readiness Tests and draws upon that experience to present techniques for reducing test bias. Nurss's chapter is not only instructive for those involved in formal test construction but also very relevant to persons who must select and interpret tests. This latter category includes nearly all teachers and parents. The checklist included in the chapter should be of particular benefit to teachers and parents because it provides an easily understood mechanism for evaluating existing instruments.

Leonard I. Jacobson

Intelligence—
Myth and Reality

Recently, I have begun to think about the role of myths in the area of intelligence. My reflections have made me wonder whether myths are really as important as we think. Perhaps our problems stem more from realities than we imagine.

I shall explain something of the history of this problem and some of its facets. The belief that the area of intelligence is filled with enduring myths seems to have begun with the publication of Hunt's (1961) influential text *Intelligence and Experience*. Hunt noted a number of myths about intelligence that he viewed as descended from two fundamental assumptions he believed to be incorrect.

The first assumption was the belief in predetermined development, that human development proceeds generally according to innate patterns predetermined by heredity. The second assumption, the belief in fixed intelligence, is essentially a correlate of the first. That

is, if development is essentially predetermined, then it follows that intelligence is essentially an unfolding of this fixed genetic potential. Hence, one would expect a generally constant and fixed intelligence quotient, particularly when maturation occurs in a benign environment that permits genetic capacity to unfold without impediment.

Now, not everything here is myth! It is not a myth but a reality that most psychologists and educators have traditionally believed these assumptions, nor is it a myth that many do today.

It should be recalled that the origins of these beliefs were present from the beginning of the mental testing movement. As early as 1904, Spearman used the newly developed approach of factor analysis to demonstrate that the pattern of correlations generated indicated the presence of a g factor. This factor was viewed as a general unitary and innate intellectual ability, and Spearman believed that he had discovered a fundamental factor underlying much of human development.

From an historical point of view, it is interesting to note that this assertion was contested from the beginning. In 1909, Thorndike, Lay, and Dean published evidence inconsistent with this view and indicating g to be a myth. Despite such early and continual criticism, the belief in intelligence as a fixed characteristic that proceeds according to genetic capacity was doubted by few until Hunt.

The intelligence testing movement has had a long and colorful history in psychology and education. During the early twentieth century, many psychologists and educators were greatly concerned with making their instruments more precise and applying their results to settings such as the schools, as well as to the shaping of public policy. The movement appears to have reached its strongest influence in 1924 with the passing of the United States Immigration Act. This law was the first ever passed in the United States in which both the findings and views of psychologists and educators played an important and perhaps decisive role (Kamin 1974).

The general position of the mental testers was the myth that science had demonstrated unequivocally that the peoples of the earth could be classified according to the merit of their genetic potential. In addition, they presented precise data to support their assertions. The methods of psychological testing demonstrated conclusively that 83 percent of the Eastern European Jews, 80 percent of the Hungarians, precisely 79 percent of the Italians, and 87 percent of the Russians were feebleminded (Kamin 1974). That these tests were administered in English to people who often did not understand the language adequately was viewed as of little importance, just as Hispano-American children are frequently given English versions of the traditional intelligence and achievement tests today in much of the United States, regardless of their skill in comprehending English.

As a result of the Immigration Act of 1924 and other legislation during the 1920s, immigration to this country by the designated "inferior peoples" was ended. The consequences of these acts were swift in coming and irrevocable. During the 1930s millions of Jews and other Europeans found themselves barred from entering the "lands of liberty" lest they further "pollute" the stock of the "indigenous" peoples. Most of these millions of rejected people eventually were murdered and their deaths are not myths either.

I recently reread the second edition of Shuey's (1966) *The Testing of Negro Intelligence,* perhaps the magnum opus of the genetic point of view and a book that is a reality and certainly no myth. It is a tour de force, filled with over five hundred pages of text and hundreds of references. The results of this scholarly work are clear. Scientific research demonstrates that there are inherent differences in the intellectual capacity of Blacks and Whites and that these differences arise from hereditary characteristics that determine the course of development. Once again we are treated to the precision of mythology in the form of scientific rigor. The difference between Blacks and Whites is a 20.3 point IQ inferiority for the Blacks.

It might be concluded from this point of view that since such differences exist one should modify the educational system to take account of these genetic differences. One way to do this would be to segregate children according to race so that each race could develop according to its own abilities. Some might think it unfortunate that there was no psychology in the nineteenth century to guide such an educational experiment properly and place it on a rational and rigorous scientific basis. Nevertheless, such a system was put into operation, and segregation is no bicentennial myth.

The traditional scientific view that intelligence represents a capacity that unfolds according to genetic potential rests on the assumption that each of the following terms can be adequately defined and measured: (1) intelligence, (2) genetic factors and their relationship to complex human behavior, and (3) intellectual capacity.

With regard to the definition of intelligence in terms of intelligence tests, the physical scientist Layzer (1974) indicated the state of this area. To this day no rational definition or quantitative representation of the intelligence factor has been proposed that has any theoretical, conceptual, or mathematical validity.

If rational or deductive accounts have failed, what of the empirical efforts to measure intelligence operationally? According to Layzer, some psychologists and educators have totally distorted the use of the operational definition in science. These definitions are presented without reference to a theoretical model or context and in a laissez faire manner in which it is impossible to assess their accuracy or adequacy. Layzer is incisive in his description of the inadequacy of intelligence tests as operational definitions of intelligence. In his words:

To measure a subject's Stanford-Binet IQ, one must administer a specific test in a specific way under specific conditions. By contrast a well-equipped physics laboratory does not need to have replicas of the standard meter and the standard kilogram to measure length and mass, and the physicist or biologist is free to devise his own tech-

niques for measuring such quantities. Systematic discrepancies between measurements of the same quantity are never ignored in the physical and biological sciences, because they signal the presence of unsuspected errors or of defects in the theory underlying the measurements. (1974, p. 1262)

Layzer goes on to analyze the differences in the use of operational definitions in physics and in the psychology of intelligence. The psychological approach fails to meet the basic standards of scientific acceptability on all counts.

The second factor, the relationship between genetics and complex human behavior, has been the subject of much recent speculation. Burt (1958, 1972) has stated that 88 percent of the variance in IQ tests results from genetic factors. Jensen (1969) has placed the figure at 80 percent. More precise mythology!

However, a number of careful analyses of the equations employed in computing heritability coefficients, such as those provided by Jensen (1969), indicate that serious problems are present in these formulations (Layzer 1974; Linn 1974; Miller and Levine 1973). In a previous paper (Jacobson 1976), I pointed out that current mathematical models of heritability assume that the variables under investigation are linear and monotonic functions that combine in an additive manner under conditions of orthogonality. Unfortunately, there is every reason to believe that these assumptions are incorrect and that nonlinear and perhaps nonmonotonic functions are present. These functions may well be capable of combining multiplicatively under conditions where covariance—and not orthogonality—occur routinely. If this is the case, heritability coefficients cannot yield correct estimates.

It would be foolish to say a priori that genetic factors are unrelated to complex human behavior and processes. But it is equally clear that if such relations do exist they are not now known. Furthermore, it will not be possible to assess this issue meaningfully until a mathematical model is devised that is adequate for the explication of these problems.

The third issue I have raised is that of defining and measuring intellectual capacity. The results of my research and those of my collaborators over the past ten years are relevant to this problem. We have viewed the results obtained from intelligence tests as indicating various types of achievement. That is, at any given age the test scores obtained may be viewed as suggestive of the extent to which a particular child has mastered various conceptual and linguistic skills valued and promoted by middle class American culture. We have used these tests as indicators of achievement and have located specific behavioral deficits, particularly for Black and Spanish-speaking preschool children. Instead of stopping here, we went further and created behavior training programs to remedy these performance problem areas.

The results of these investigations have been reported in numerous journals (Greeson and Jacobson 1973; Jacobson, Berger, Bergman, Millham, and Greeson 1971; Jacobson, Bernal, Greeson, Rich, and Millham 1973; Jacobson, Bernal, Lopez, Morrison, and Anderson, in press; Jacobson and Greeson 1972; Jacobson, Kellogg, Greeson, and Bernal 1973) and indicate that intelligence test scores may be raised greatly as a function of participation in these programs. In one study reported (Jacobson, Berger, Bergman, Millham, and Greeson 1971), we placed preschool, predominately Black children from poverty backgrounds in a training program for conceptual acquisition. Within twenty hours, the children mastered the program.

The initially low IQ subjects increased their Stanford-Binet IQ's the most, with a mean increase of 20.67 points across conditions, a figure disturbingly close to Shuey's. In the low IQ-modeling condition, the increase was over 30 points. For the entire modeling condition, the average child's IQ increased from the dull-normal to the upper portion of the average range of intellectual functioning, as a result of participation in the program.

Similarly, intelligence test scores have been found to be responsive to programs that systematically teach language (Greeson and Jacobson 1971; Jacobson, Bernal, Lopez, Morrison and Anderson 1976) or that provide social interaction experiences in the absence of teaching (Jacobson, Berger, Bergman, Millham, and Greeson 1971).

One may conclude from these and similar studies that if intelligence test scores are direct measures of intellectual capacity then this capacity is among the most mercurial, unstable, and transitory factors discovered to date. A more logical conclusion would be that the tests currently employed have no demonstrable relationship to this assumed intellectual capacity.

CONCLUSIONS

It is reasonable to conclude that intelligence has not been adequately defined, that the relationship of genetic factors to complex human behavior is still unknown, and that the belief that intelligence tests measure cognitive, behavioral, or genetic capacity is false. These conclusions are realities and not myths.

In a recent review of Kamin's (1974) text, the geneticist Lewontin (1976) indicated that with regard to the relationship of intelligence to behavior genetics we have learned more about the conduct of research in this area than about the actual relations that may exist. What we have discovered "is a pattern of shoddiness, carelessness, miserable experimental design, misreporting, and misrepresentation amounting to a major scandal" (Lewontin 1976, p. 97).

Lewontin states that it is not possible to approach this topic "without a sense of indignation and of shame at the distortion of science that has gone on under the label of human behavioral genetics." He concludes that it "is time now for the field to purge itself and to reassert its claim to honest scholarship" (1976, p. 98).

The perversion of science into racism is no myth. The history of twentieth century racism in the form of many of the allegedly scientific studies of intelligence and heritability is still all too real and very much with us. Perhaps the time for "honest scholarship" has arrived to wash away centuries of the reality of racism so that someday it will be remembered only as myth.

ACKNOWLEDGEMENTS

I would like to acknowledge the kind assistance of Timothy J. Alper, Javier Lasaga, and Ana Mari Cauce.

References

Burt, C. "Inheritance of General Intelligence." *American Psychologist* 27 (1972): 175-190.

Burt, C. "The Inheritance of Mental Ability." *American Psychologist* 13 (1958): 1-15.

Greeson, L. E., and Jacobson, L. I. "A Behavior Modification Approach to Programming Language Acquisition of Children from Poverty Backgrounds." In *Advances in Behavior Therapy, Volume 4*, edited by R. D. Rubin, J. P. Brady, and J. D. Henderson, pp. 55-65. New York: Academic Press, 1973.

Greeson, L. E., and Jacobson, L. I. "Effects of Modeling Language Units of Differing Complexity on the Language Acquisition of Preschool Black Children." *Proceedings of the 79th Annual Convention of the American Psychological Association* 6 (1971): 197-198.

Hunt, J. McV. *Intelligence and Experience.* New York: Ronald Press, 1961.

Jacobson, L. I. "Genetic Correlations, Squared or Unsquared: Can They Be Accurately Computed?" Unpublished manuscript, 1976.

Jacobson, L. I.; Berger, S. E.; Bergman, R. L.; Millham, J.; and Greeson, L. E. "Effects of Age, Sex, Systematic Conceptual Learning, Acquisition of Learning Sets, and Programmed Social Interaction on the Intellectual and Conceptual Development of Preschool Children from Poverty Backgrounds." *Child Development* 42 (1971): 1399-1415.

Jacobson, L. I.; Bernal, G.; Greeson, L. E.; Rich, J. J.; and Millham, J. "Intellectual and Conceptual Acquisition in Retarded Children: A Follow-up Study." *Bulletin of the Psychonomic Society* 1 (1973): 340-342.

Jacobson, L. I.; Bernal, G.; Lopez, G. N.; Morrison, A.; and Anderson, C. L. "La Modification du Comportement et l'Acquisition du Langage chez les Enfants Noirs de Familles Pauvres." *Revue Internationale de Psychologie Appliquée,* in press.

Jacobson, L. I., and Greeson, L. E. "Effects of Systematic Conceptual Learning on the Intellectual Development of Preschool Children from Poverty Backgrounds: A Follow-up Study." *Child Development* 43 (1972): 1111-1115.

Jacobson, L. I.; Kellogg, R. W.; Greeson, L. E.; and Bernal, G. "Programming the Intellectual and Conceptual Development of Retarded Children with Behavioral Techniques." In *Advances in Behavior Therapy, Volume 4,* edited by R. D. Rubin, J. P. Brady, and J. D. Henderson, pp. 13-20. New York: Academic Press, 1973.

Jensen, A. R. "How Much Can We Boost IQ and Scholastic Achievement?" *Harvard Educational Review* 39 (1969) 1-123.

Kamin, L. J. *The Science and Politics of IQ.* New York: Halsted Press, 1974.

Layzer, D. "Heritability Analyses of IQ Scores: Science or Numerology?" *Science* 183 (1974): 1259-1266.

Lewontin, R. C. "Review of L. J. Kamin, 'The Science and Politics of IQ.' " *Contemporary Psychology* 21 (1976): 97-98.

Linn, R. L. "Unsquared Genetic Correlations." *Psychological Bulletin* 81 (1974): 203-206.

Miller, J.K., and Levine, D. "Correlation Between Genetically Matched Groups Versus Reliability Theory: A Reply to Jensen." *Psychological Bulletin* 79 (1973) 142-144.

Shuey, A. M. *The Testing of Negro Intelligence.* 2nd ed. New York: Social Science Press, 1966.

Spearman, C. " 'General Intelligence,' Objectively Determined and Measured." *American Journal of Psychology* 15 (1904): 201-293.

Thorndike, E. L.; Lay, W.; and Dean, P. R. "The Relation of Accuracy in Sensory Discrimination to General Intelligence." *American Journal of Psychology* 20 (1909) 364-369.

Joanne R. Nurss

An Attempt to Reduce Test Bias In Readiness Tests

Readiness tests were developed in the 1930s as a measure of a child's readiness for school learning. The concept of readiness then was one of psychological and mental preparedness for first grade instruction. It was a unitary concept, primarily developmental rather than educational. Children who were judged not ready for first grade instruction were removed from the instructional group to give them more time to develop. Early readiness tests measured skills very similar to those measured by verbal aptitude tests (Durkin 1976).

Since the thirties, the concept of readiness has changed drastically. Gradually, it was broken down into component skills, such as vocabulary, verbal comprehension, visual discrimination, copying, auditory discrimination, and number concepts. Primary teachers began to incorporate these skills into the first grade curriculum, believing that they could be taught or, at least, practiced. For a time, all children entering first grade had a six-week period of readiness instruction, even if they could already read!

Readiness tests have become a measure of the child's current progress in developing a variety of skills related to the beginning reading process, not a measure of innate mental aptitude. They assume a continuous, on-going development of prereading skills, giving the teacher and parents an assessment of where each child is on the skill's continuum. It is at that point that instruction begins. This concept of readiness testing also assumes that an assessment of individual skills (or skills grouped within one skill area, such as visual or auditory) provides more valid, important instructional information than does a global measure of the child's overall functioning. The first step in devising this type of test is to analyze the beginning reading process and to determine which skills are necessary for success.

Current readiness tests must also be appropriate for all young children, not just White, middle socioeconomic status, suburban children. It is not possible to develop a "culture-free" test; however, anything that obviously or consistently discriminates against any group of children because of their race, sex, ethnic group, language background, geographical region, socioeconomic level, or community size must be eliminated. The goal is to construct a test that measures a child's level of prereading skills compared to a nationwide population and provides instructional information for the teacher. Thus, the test remains oriented to the school situation, an essentially middle socioeconomic institution in America.

The points discussed below are aspects of the development of a readiness test. Consideration is given to ways to reduce test bias and examples are given from the 1976 revision of the *Metropolitan Readiness Tests* (Nurss and McGauvran).

CONTENT ANALYSIS

The first task is to select measures of skills related to beginning reading such as auditory discrimination, rhyming, phoneme-grapheme correspondence, visual matching, visual part-whole discrimination, and language comprehension. Obvious measures of general intelligence and culture such as vocabulary and items with a heavy memory load can be eliminated in favor of items measuring specific reading-related skills. If longer language items are repeated, they are more likely to measure language than memory. The *Metropolitan Readiness Tests* (MRT) include tests of reading-related auditory and visual skills such as discrimination of beginning consonants and visual matching of words and letters. Also included are language comprehension measures of the child's understanding of grammatical structures and short passages requiring the child to draw inferences and integrate orally-presented information.

PICTURES

Pictures that illustrate objects, concepts, activities, and experiences common to all children are less likely to be biased. If pictures balance urban/rural and geographic areas, children familiar with only one area of the country are not penalized. A balance of race, sex, and ethnic groups should be maintained in the illustrations and in the names of children and adults. Pictures can avoid stereotypes of sex-typed activities by illustrations such as boys cooking and girls doing woodworking. Wherever possible in the MRT, the pictures of the stimulus and options are named before the item task is given and the same illustration of an object or animal is repeated throughout the test.

VOCABULARY AND DIALECT

To avoid vocabulary bias, word lists of the oral vocabulary of preschool children may be used so that only words thought to be generally familiar to all children are selected. Studies of Black English, Appalachian dialect, and Spanish describe language sounds not familiar to these native speakers. Any phonemes, phoneme-grapheme correspondences, or phoneme-positions not familiar to these speakers can be avoided in auditory subtests. Teachers are cautioned to use the MRT only with children who are bilingual or who have acquired minimal fluency in English. Information is given indicating ways to use the school language subtests to assist children in comprehending standard school dialect, not to judge or penalize them.

ITEM BIAS

In an effort to reduce item bias, a chi-square technique (Scheuneman 1975) has been devised to ascertain if significant differences in item scores exist between two population groups with the same subtest score. Tests are made at various score levels. Items may be assessed in this fashion for possible bias against Blacks or Whites, boys or girls. This technique was used to identify any biased items in the MRT so they might be eliminated. These included both easily explained items such as negative grammatical structures (biased against Blacks) and less easily explained items (several of which were biased against Whites).

STANDARDIZATION

Use of U.S. census data to select communities and schools within communities by geographical location, size of community, and socio-economic level produces a balanced national standardization sample. For a prereading test, children must be included from parochial, large city, suburban, independent, and rural school systems, as well as from systems with no public kindergarten programs. The MRT was standardized on a stratified random sample of nearly 69,000 children, including a sample from large cities that allowed development of special large city norms.

TEST REVIEW

Assuming that adults in the various ethnic and geographic groups mentioned would be the best "judges" of whether or not a test is "fair" for children in their group, teachers, parents, and professionals in early childhood education, psychology, and linguistics can review the tests

tive self-concepts, all agree that the self is formed through interaction with "others." Negative self-evaluation logically follows, then, after interaction with significant others who deprecate personal traits. Since this element (the concept of the significant other) is crucial to previous explanations of negative self-concept, we employed a modified version of Mulford's Significant Others Test (SOT) to operationalize the concept of reference categories (Mulford 1955; Denzin 1972; Moore, Schmitt, and Grupp 1973). Our nodified version of the SOT contained six numbered lines for response and read as follows:

Please make a list of those people or groups of people whose opinion of you as a person *concern you the most. Give only the relationship to you, and not their names: for example, father, best friend, minister, etc. . . .*

While the construct validity of this test has not been demonstrated, it has "face validity." It is assumed (1) that the others mentioned correspond to the subject's perception of those who are significant for their behavior, (2) that respondents are conscious of the others who are influencing their behavior, and (3) that the youth's most important others are also the most salient and therefore will be mentioned on the protocol.

CODING: TST AND SOT

A number of coding manuals have been developed for the TST (Spitzer, Couch, and Stratton 1972). Content analysis of the TST responses here involved distribution of each line item into one of five corresponding hierarchically organized categories: self-evaluations, ideological statements or beliefs, ambitions, statements of interests, and finally, those related to social groups and classifications. In short, this scheme examines where the respondents place themselves in the social system, their rationale or perspective on this social structure, and their place in it. It also examines affects pertaining to social objects as well as personal assessment of role playing.

Protocols were futher coded in terms of "con-

sensuality." Consensual statements are objective statements by individuals about themselves that require no further explanation and which can be verified, e.g., "I am fourteen years old." Subconsensual statements refer to norms that may vary and about which the analyst would have to question the respondent in order to understand the subjective frame of reference. These two codes involved both the number of these statements made as well as the proportion of the total number of statements they comprise.

Finally, TST protocols were coded for self-derogation using Kuhn's "Procedure for Assessing Disturbance on the TST" (Spitzer, Couch, and Stratton 1972). Three themes in self-derogation are identified by this procedure: derogation of self, derogation of other social objects (persons, situations, values, etc.) and conflicting or contradictory attitudes toward the self. A dichotomous classification for derogation was employed (yes or no) based on the following criteria:

1. One severely self-derogating statement (e.g., "I am a failure");

2. The presence of two or more less severely derogating self-statements ("I try to impress people too much," or "I'm too social");

3. Three or more specific skill derogations;

4. One severely derogating statement about valued social objects; and/or

5. One sweeping contradiction.

Coding for the SOT protocol simply involved distribution of responses into ten major categories of others drawn from the study population as well as previous research—family others, siblings, peers, friends, teachers, religious others, social groups, the community, work references, and a residual category (Denzin 1972; Moore, Schmitt, and Grupp 1973).

Finally, for a measure of socioeconomic status, the Hollingshead Two-Factor Index was used employing data from both parents. This index is based on the differential weighting of education (by a factor of four) and occupation (by a factor of seven). The cases are distributed among five classes (Hollingshead and Redlich 1958). The first class roughly corresponds to the traditional upper socioeconomic status, that is, professionals, executives, managers of large firms. Class II corresponds to the upper-middle socioeconomic status, including professionals, administrative personnel, and small business owners. Class III, the lower-middle socioeconomic status, contains white-collar personnel, sales and clerical workers. Class IV is the working socioeconomic status comprised of skilled and semiskilled manual workers, while Class V is lower socioeconomic status including unskilled workers, domestics, and laborers.

The relationships between these concepts will be analyzed using contingency tables (cross-tabulation). The significance of differences obtained is evaluated through use of the chi-square statistic, while the strength of the associations observed will be evaluated by the Contingency Coefficient (C).

LIMITATIONS[2]

Given the sensitive nature of this area of research and the often controversial nature of findings, it is important to explicitly review the limits of the data at hand. First, given high "dropout rates," minority students may be underrepresented in the sample. Analysis of the relationship between race and grades in our sample supports this possibility.[3] Blacks also reported

slightly more days out from school for health and nonhealth reasons than did Whites. These points should be kept in mind when evaluating Black/White comparisons below.

Secondly, the TST and the SOT and the questions pertaining to mother's and father's education and occupation were all placed near the end of the questionnaire, with the result that these items were left incomplete by respondents or were illegible. This reduced the ultimate working N to 886, due to the cumulative combination of missing items. It is difficult to interpret the significance of noncompletion rates. Student response to the questionnaire was generally very favorable since it involved questions dealing with popular teen centers such as the Free Medical Clinic and other drop-in centers. Comparison of "non-ascertainedness" by race, class, and grades showed no substantial differences in the backgrounds of the two groups. We might argue that one implication of the law of large numbers might be that we should expect that the net effect of numerous trivial or frivolous reasons for nonresponse produce a chance effect, effectively cancelling each other out.

FINDINGS

An unusual and unexpected result of analysis of the TST responses is that the two major racial groups (Black and White; other races were dropped from analysis due to small N's) do not exhibit differential patterns of response. There were no significant differences in number of responses by race. Relatively the same proportions of Blacks and Whites mentioned the categories of self-evaluations, ideological beliefs, ambitions, interests, and social group classifications.[4] Although this finding has been reported

---

[2]Most of the severe limitations apparent in previous research in this area have been counterbalanced in this study. Two of the most serious limits, for example, have been the relatively small N's of previous studies (Hauser 1971) and the nonrandomness of samples (Grier and Cobbs 1968). One "classic" (Kardiner and Ovessey 1952), for example, was based on a sample of 25 persons, half of whom were patients of the two psychiatrists!

[3]In comparing grades by race, a significant chi-square (19.1, df=3) was obtained. However, the association was relatively weak (C=.12), and in the bottom category (mostly D's and F's) more Whites (4 percent) reported low grades than Blacks (3 percent). The association between grades and socioeconomic status is much stronger (chi-square = 55.38, df=12, p<.001, C=.23), suggesting that both Whites and Blacks are equally vulnerable to underrepresentation in the sample.

---

[4]The team which evaluated these protocols was biracial. It was surprising how similar the two study groups were in their use of language. Of course the TST elicits only brief sentences, and more complex differences in syntax or logic perhaps remain latent. As a check on coding reliability a blind subsamples of both TST and SOT were recorded by a second set of workers, with replication values of .95 and .94 respectively obtained.

previously (Wellman 1969), the major thrust of intergroup thought would seem to suggest a somewhat different pattern of response for the Black identity. Perhaps this is a result of interest in differences (with resultant magnification) as opposed to similarities between the two groups.

A provocative reversal of previous findings is apparent in the analysis of derogation by race (Table 1). Significantly more Whites than Blacks presented self-derogating protocols! While the relationship is only moderately strong (C = .17), the percentage difference is substantial.

Table 1. Self-Derogation and Race (N = 988)

Self-Derogating Response	Race	
	Black	White
No	73%	54%
	(n = 218)	(n = 375)
Yes	27%	46%
	(n = 82)	(n = 313)

$X^2 = 27.96$, p < .001; C = .17

It would seem likely that this finding reflects the effect of the rising Black awareness movement. Banks and Grambs (1972) have argued that the Black revolt *has not* significantly changed the self-concepts and evaluations of most Black children and youth. This conclusion is somewhat jaded by the size difference reported here in level of derogation. However, we are obviously not in a position to conclude that certain programs or movements have *reduced* derogation among Blacks since we are unable to ascertain the extent to which other developments (e.g., increased interracial competition) may have boosted the self-derogation of Whites.

More importantly, several major arguments regarding Black self-derogation have emphasized the importance of socioeconomic status and cultural oppressive effects. Cross-tabulation of self-derogation by socioeconomic status, however, reveals *no significant differences in derogation* (Table 2)!

Table 2. Self-Derogation and Socioeconomic Status (N = 886)

Self-Derogating Response	Socioeconomic Status				
	I	II	III	IV	V
No	55%	60%	62%	59%	56%
	(54)	(61)	(115)	(186)	(104)
Yes	45%	40%	38%	41%	44%
	(45)	(41)	(70)	(127)	(83)

$X^2 = 2.48$, N.S.; C = .05

When race and socioeconomic status of respondent are simultaneously controlled, however, an interesting specification of the conditional nature of the original relationship between race and self-derogation is obtained (Table 3) (for discussion of specification, see Rosenberg 1968). Significant differences between Black and White respondents appear *only* among lower-middle and working socioeconomic status youth. The strength of the original relationship holds for the middle socioeconomic status youth, while the association is strengthened in the working socioeconomic status (C = .24)!

We cannot assert that one group is "high" or "low" in derogation without identifying an arbitrary "pathology," but, it would seem that derogation is least serious among middle and working socioeconomic status Blacks. It would be more parsimonious, then, to explain this two-cell discrepancy by pointing to the effects of various social action groups in those population groups rather than to explain the overall higher rates among remaining categories of both Blacks and Whites. This is indeed a surprising finding, however, given the fact that the initial locus of the awareness movement was among upper socioeconomic status Blacks who exhibit here comparatively high levels of self-derogation.

Table 3. Respondents with Self-Derogating Responses by Race and Socioeconomic Status, % (N)

Socioeconomic Status	Race Black	White	χ²	Association
I	43% (7)	46% (91)	.05 N.S.	C = .02
II	35% (17)	41% (85)	.03 N.S.	C = .04
III	23% (47)	43% (138)	4.79 p < .02	C = .17
IV	26% (120)	50% (191)	17.20 p > .001	C = .24
V	36% (61)	48% (123)	1.89 N.S.	C = .11

Table 4. Mention of Reference Categories and Race*

Category of Reference Other Mentioned	Race Black	White	χ²	Association
Family	86%	87%	.34 N.S.	C = .02
Siblings	51%	43%	6.02 p < .01	C = .07
Peers	3%	7%	6.9 p < .01	C = .08
Friends	67%	69%	20.6 N.S.	C = .02
Teachers	13%	24%	15.3 p < .001	C = .12
Religious Others	11%	12%	.16 N.S.	C = .01
Social Groups	1%	3%	3.9 N.S.	C = .07
Community References	10%	11%	.12 N.S.	C = .01
Work	4%	5%	.29 N.S.	C = .02
Residual Category	2%	5%	3.6 N.S.	C = .06

*Percentages do not total 100 since each line represents part of a different table, i.e., Family, mentioned (86%), not mentioned (14%), by race of respondent.

Most of the significant others mentioned are *primary others* —representing relationships with sources in primary groups, mainly the family and close friends. This suggests that school personnel and other abstractly significant others (i.e., significant by virtue of status or position) are not only subjectively selected out, they are also temporally irrelevant to the interactions that establish the self and its sources of self-esteem. Kuhn's concept of the orientational other (a basic source of identity) and Denzin's notion of the role-specific other (important because of and within specific roles) is instructive here (Schmitt 1972). Teachers who represent a possible threat to self-esteem are basically limited in influence to geographically isolated role performances. Arnold Rose's question "What other?" persists (Rosenberg 1973) since the relationship between self and other reflects both objective and subjective elements of role adaptation which cannot be predicted without consulting the student.

REFERENCE GROUPS: What "Others" and Why?

Given the relative similarity of self-statements made by the two groups, we turn now to analysis of the theoretical source of those statements (Table 4). Again, with few exceptions, we see similar patterns of choice of reference others with one significant exception. Whites are more likely to mention teachers and school others and less likely to mention siblings than are Black students. This may hold some importance for the interpretation of the substantive importance of lower rates of self-derogation among Blacks. Given the lower pattern of grade achievement reported by Black students as compared to Whites, it is not surprising that Blacks would be less likely to *select* significant others who threaten self-esteem with negative evaluation.

A more important pattern of responses is also evident in Table 4.

DISCUSSION

The image of Black youth suffering from flat egos apparently forms the basis of a widespread myth with significant policy implications. The plethora of social action programs that use the depressed self-concept as an axis of intervention, then, are without foundation if these findings can be replicated. More importantly, the image of pathologically malformed Black self-concepts functions as a powerful antilocution (Kurakawa 1971) that determines the image of this group to other competing groups. This image apparently *doesn't* function as a self-fulfilling prophecy for *most* Black youth (the possibly serious deleterious effect on some individuals should not be overlooked!). Yet this myth is detrimental to the esteem in which this group is placed by the rest of the society and the way in which that society responds to this group.

Educational policies that focus on the flat ego as a fulcrum for reversing undesirable learning trends would seem to be theoretically doomed. Arguments over whether self-concept or self-concept of ability leads to grade achievement or the reverse (Wilson 1969, p. 48) are irrelevant if teachers and school others are temporally seriate to the processes that form self-concept. Thus their influence can only be segmental and limited to those whose selves are already susceptible (receptive) to school influence. These students are probably not the ones whose rates of learning are problematic.

These findings would suggest, however, that programmic responses that utilize significant others as a basis for reaching problem learners should prove effective if the correct others are identified and effectively contacted. Thomas et al. (1969) attempted to use *parents* in this manner (parental evaluations and expectations were experimentally raised to see if there was an increase in school achievement). They were surprised to learn that many parents rejected an ascribed role as significant other, that parents tended to blame teachers, lazy children, and boring reading material rather than accept responsibility for their personal influence, and that parents were often hostile and defensive, often asserting that their child's school performance was none of their business (1969, pp. 58-59). Our findings suggest, then, that the links between significant other and school behavior are far more important than the links between self-concept and learning. This would seem to form a social psychological basis, then, for increased school-family coordination. This research was supported by a grant from the greater Cleveland Associated Foundations, administered through the Administration of Justice Committee of the Governmental Research Institute, Cleveland, Ohio. The author wishes to thank Professors Marie R. Haug, Stephen Swadley, Roy G. Francis, and Bruce Cameron for their help and insights.

References

Ausubel, D.P., and Ausubel, P. "Ego Development among Segregated Negro Children." In *Education in Depressed Areas,* edited by A. Y. Passow, pp. 109-141. New York: Teachers College, Columbia University, 1963.

Banks, J. A., and Grambs, J. D., eds. *Black Self-Concept.* New York: McGraw-Hill, 1972.

Clark, K. *Dark Ghetto: Dilemmas of Social Problems.* New York: Harper & Row, 1965.

Coleman, J. S.; Campbell, E.; Hosson, C.; McPartland, J.; Moon, A.; Weisfeld, F.; and York, R. *Equality of Educational Opportunity.* Washington, D.C.: U.S. Government Printing Office, 1964.

Denzin, K. "The Significant Others of a College Population." In *Symbolic Interaction: A Reader in Social Psychology,* edited by J. G. Manis and B. N. Meltzer. Boston: Allyn and Bacon, 1972.

Dreger, R. M., and Miller, K. "Comparative Psychological Studies of Negroes and Whites in the United States." *Psychological Bulletin* 57 (1960): 361.

Erikson, E. "The Concept of Identity in Race Relations: Notes and Queries." In *The Negro American,* edited by T. Parsons and K. Clark, pp. 227-253. Boston: Beacon Press, 1965.

Fanon, F. *Black Skin, White Face.* New York: Grove Press, 1967.

Greenberg, J. W. "Comments on Self-Perceptions of Disadvantaged Children." *American Educational Research Journal* 7 (1970): 627-630.

Greenwald, H., and Oppenheim, D. "Reported Magnitude of Self-Misidentification among Negro Children: Artifact?" *Journal of Personality and Social Psychology* 8 (1968): 49-52.

Grier, W., and Cobbs, P. *Black Rage.* New York: Bantam Books, 1968.

Hauser, S. *Black and White Identity Formation.* New York: John Wiley & Sons, 1971.

Havelick, R. S., Jr., and Vane, J. R. "Race, Competency and Level of Achievement: Relationship to Modeling in Elementary School Children." *Journal of Psychology* 87 (1974): 23-28.

Hollingshead, A. B., and Redlich, F. C. *Social Class and Mental Illness.* New York: John Wiley & Sons, 1958.

Kardiner, A., and Ovessey, D. *The Mark of Oppression.* New York: W. W. Norton & Co., 1952.

Kuhn, M. H. "Self Attitudes by Age, Sex, and Professional Training." *Sociological Quarterly* 1 (1960): 39-55.

Kuhn, M. H., and McPartland, T. S. "An Empirical Investigation of Self Attitudes." *American Sociological Review* 19 (1954): 68-76.

Kurakawa, M. "Mutual Perceptions of Racial Images: White, Black, and Japanese Americans." *Journal of Social Issues* 27, no. 4 (1971): 213-236.

Ledvinka, J. "Race of Interviewer and the Language Elaboration of Black Interviewees." *Journal of Social Issues* 27, no. 4 (1971): 185-198.

Moore, H. A.; Schmitt, R. L.; and Grupp, S. E. "Observations on the Role Specific and Orientational Other." *Pacific Sociological Review* 16, no. 3 (July 1973): 509.

Mulford, H. A. "Toward an Instrument to Identify and Measure the Self, Significant Others, and Alcohol in the Symbolic Environment." Ph.D. dissertation, State University of Iowa, 1955.

Pettigrew, T. *A Profile of the Negro American.* Princeton, N.J.: Van Nostrand, 1964.

Rosenberg, M. *The Logic of Survey Analysis.* New York: Basic Books, 1968.

Rosenberg, M. *Society and Adolescent Self-Image.* Princeton, N.J.: Princeton University Press, 1965.

Rosenberg, M. "Which Significant Others?" *American Behavioral Scientist* 16, no. 6 (1973): 52.

Schmitt, R. L. "Major Role Change and Self Change." *Sociological Quarterly* 7, no. 3 (1966): 311.

Schmitt, R. L. *The Reference Other Orientation: An Extension of the Reference Group Concept.* Carbondale, Ill.: Southern Illinois University Press, 1972.

Soares, A., and Soares, L. "Self-Perceptions of Culturally Disadvantaged Children." *American Educational Research Journal* 6 (1969): 31-45.

Spitzer, S.; Couch, C.; and Stratton, J. *The Assessment of the Self.* Iowa City, Iowa: Sernoll, 1972.

Spitzer, S., and Stratton, J. "The Self Concept: Test Equivalence and Perceived Validity." *Sociological Quarterly* 7 (1966): 665-680.

Thomas, S.; Brookover, W. B.; LePere, J. M.; Hamachek, D. E.; and Erickson, E. L. "An Experiment to Modify Self-Concept and School Performance." *Sociological Focus* 3, no. 1 (1969): 55.

Wellman, B. "A Study of Self-Conception of Negro and White Youths." Ph.D. dissertation, Harvard University, 1969.

Wilson, A. B. *The Consequences of Segregation: Academic Achievement in a Northern Community.* Berkeley, Calif.: Glendessary Press, 1969.

Zirkel, P. "Self Concept and the 'Disadvantage' of Ethnic Group Membership and Mixture." *Review of Educational Research* 41 (1971): 211-225.

Zirkel, P., and Moss, E. "Self Concept and Ethnic Group Membership among Public School Students." *American Educational Research Journal* 8 (1971): 253-265.

John R. Dill

Toward a Developmental Theory of the Inner-City Child

It has been long established that children's behavior is greatly influenced by the surrounding environment. It is also known that environmental conditions and experiences will determine the attitudes, competencies, values, and skills that are formed during the important developmental years. Yet the fact that children's behavior is adaptable attests to the almost infinite malleability of human behavioral potential and the important interaction of the genetic-environmental matrix.

The developmental psychologist's concern with environmental factors does not indicate a deliberate subordination of genetic contributions to behavioral development. The majority of developmentalists recognize, in varying degrees of emphasis, the importance of hereditary factors. Knowledge about environmental influences, however, provides the behavioral scientist with the vehicle to conduct direct observations and make appropriate manipulations of subcomponents of the environment. The

psychologist-scientist can thus arrive at a further understanding of the intricate dynamics of children's behavior. The psychologist-therapist, in attempting to arrive at the underpinnings of maladaptive child behavior, engages in this same process.

While such advances in the field of psychology are broadly recognized, there presently does not exist a cogent body of knowledge, investigative methods, or a systematic theory about inner-city children who have often been perceived as pathological, deviant, and deficient. Such is the case when inner-city children are portrayed as being fatherless, verbally incompetent, and inadequately socialized. This pejorative stance will neither advance our knowledge base nor provide the mechanisms for facilitating equitable human development. These goals can only be attained through the systematic formulation of a theory concerned with the behavioral development of inner-city children.

THE ROLE OF THE ENVIRONMENT

Many of the current concepts about environmental influences on children's development can be traced to the seventeenth century British philosopher John Locke, whose concept of *tabula rasa* depicted the child as a passive recipient of environmental forces. Although Locke's notions have been greatly modified and enhanced by modern theory and research, the original concept, which is the basis of empiricism, still remains a potent force in developmental psychology (Langer 1969). Virtually all of the child's attributes, belief systems, cognitive abilities, and other behaviors are now believed to be influenced by the environment. Of course, genetic factors also contribute significantly to these attributes and behaviors.

Quantitative and qualitative attributes of the environment must be considered as well. Quantitatively, it is generally posited that the child who experiences a dearth of environmental stimulation (either physical or social) will be impaired, often irreversibly. Whether such findings have any direct significance to socioeconomic status (SES) will be considered later.

Study of the qualitative level of environment emphasizes the nature of existing organizations, institutions, and functions: a society composed of people, institutions, norms, and values. Within the context of contemporary American society, major considerations must include the prevailing system of social stratification based on the differentiation of economic resources, occupational prestige, educational opportunity, and political power. For developing children, such a social structure means that behaviors are acquired within the limitations of their family's SES. Yet the socialization process in contemporary America is not that straightforward. Instead of children's experiences being defined in relation to their cultural setting, centralized and desirable norms of childrearing and child behavior are most often imposed by society. Middle SES existence has thus been considered normative, while any other SES has been labeled deviant, especially if that SES is in the lower end of the social stratum.

It may seem odd that an intrinsically differentiated society such as America does not tolerate a diversity of life-styles, mores, value systems, and methods for childhood socialization and development. However, this intolerance reflects the "melting-pot" thesis which promotes an orientation toward "a presumably single dominating pattern of norms of the nation; it does not encourage maintenance of permanent, pluralistic social, cultural and political structures" (Hess 1970, p. 549). While what is "good, appropriate and desirable" is therefore defined, this system does not indicate how such norms are to be attained. These goals can apparently only be reached by people with economic and educational accessibility. Inequality has its strongest impact here, in that certain groups of parents and children often do not have the freedom of choice to change their way of life, even if they have the inclination to do so. Low SES parents are often limited in their pursuit to better the lives of their children.

THE INNER-CITY EXPERIENCE

Antecedents to inner-city children's behavior must be examined within the context of their social milieu, whether that milieu is portrayed as a culture of poverty or a social system of cultural adaptational patterns (Leacock 1971). From either viewpoint, such a life-style is not one of personal choice. This issue is further compounded when ethnicity enters the picture; many behavioral patterns of Black children may reflect the interaction of adaptational behaviors and socially transmitted cultural traditions. We need to understand how these factors operate.

Various dimensions of inner-city behavior can have direct influences on childhood socialization, for example, a sense of powerlessness, vulnerability to disaster, restrictive alternatives, and disparity in prestige (Allen 1970). However, the distinction between true cultural traditions and adaptational styles has not been made. Are Black parenting styles derived from African origins, evolutionary New World adaptations, or both?

A brief examination of the sense of powerlessness will illustrate the complexity of these issues. The powerless parent may often transmit this orientation to the child, who then may express it as dependency or passivity when confronted with conflict. Alternative behaviors or attitudes which may be manifested are low self-esteem, nonassertiveness, or high conformity.

Other familial and parenting patterns can also contribute to inner-city children's behavior. Economic privations do not necessarily imply an impoverished culture. Low SES parents often realize short- and long-range educational goals for themselves and their children. These families' value systems may include rewards for achievement. Such families may be characterized by economic stability, as the parents are often able to effectively conquer the bureaucratic morass of social service agencies, health clinics, and the school system. Such social skills are invariably transmitted to children who often become high achievers, adapt better to school, and are able to cope with social and economic realities.

Parent-child systems may also be strongly influenced by a sex factor. Girls may especially benefit from their mothers' talents, and boys from their fathers' talents. Much more substantive research is needed in these areas.

Diversity and heterogeneity, as we have seen, exist within family settings and the resulting child behaviors. What factors precede this process of socialization in the inner-city family? Why do two sets of parents from similar SES settings implement dissimilar socialization experiences which result in different childhood behaviors? The parents' own developmental experiences at two critical points may be important: (1) their own developmental years, and (2) the time prior to parenthood.

Several vital issues must be addressed in understanding the importance of the parents' experiences. A number of social indexes might be used to examine various aspects of inner-city socialization practices and resulting child behaviors. One area of study should be the development of a better understanding of the economic-behavioral processes involved. For example, the very poor rural family who moves to an urban setting is perhaps exhibiting maladaptive patterns to the former hostile environment. Adaptational styles of other families may be more positive.

The role of adult models in the parents' own formative years must be considered, too. I interviewed one successful low-income Black man who discussed the transmission of the attribute of tenacity from his grandfather to his father to him. Another man's grandmother was a "matriarch" who modeled an effective adaptational approach to her offspring. The absence of such positive and powerful role models might affect the development of the child's positive adaptational behaviors.

Social adaptational indicators (tangible and intangible experiences and persons which influence an individual) are a third consideration. The mediator may be another person who influ-

ences a parent or a work-related experience which alters the parents' values. Such factors are usually effective because the individual was predisposed to change.

Trends of success/failure that appear among family members are another area in which more research is needed. From casual observations, I have been impressed by cases of both inconsistency and consistency among siblings. Sometimes only a few family members attain a level of stability or success, while in other cases success is consistent across all siblings.

These and other factors represent distinctive differences in the process of development of inner-city children when compared to middle SES children because a greater number of antecedent variables can influence inner-city children's behavior. Middle SES children's experiences could be called consonant experiences, implying that the parents' higher educational and occupational prestige provides a fairly well-defined course of developmental experiences. This does not negate the possibility that the low SES child can achieve upward mobility, but emphasizes that change in socioeconomic status is possible. Children from both backgrounds may be destined for a middle SES lifestyle, but middle SES children obviously have better opportunities to realize this goal, although the middle SES child will not necessarily reach this social level because of inheritance. Also, it is not unusual that the middle SES experiences, especially in first generation middle SES Black families, lead to rejection of this value system. This phenomenon requires exhaustive examination.

THE INNER-CITY CHILD'S BEHAVIOR— A RESEARCH REVIEW

The bulk of research on inner-city children has focused on three areas: personality (self-concept), language ability (nonstandard English), and cognitive functioning (intelligence test performance). There is no question in my mind that the emphasis on these three areas represents political concerns rather than purely behavioral science interests.

Research on Black children's self-concept originated with the pioneering work of Kenneth and Mamie Clark (1940). Black children were shown Black and White dolls and asked to assign positive or negative traits to the dolls. The children tended to select White dolls for positive traits and Black dolls for negative traits. The children also tended to deny the similarity between themselves and the Black dolls. Later research in this area has generally supported these findings although various subtleties have been noted. For instance, recent evidence indicates that the nature of the parent-child relationship, sex, intelligence, and a host of other variables are important correlates to the child's racial identity (Porter 1971; Silverstein and Krate 1975). Black children's self-concepts may also be changing since some studies have shown that Black children show a preference for Black dolls. This literature seems to imply that one of the major problems of Black children is self-identity. The psychoeducational implications of this notion are obvious: school achievement, social adjustment, and economic success all hinge on the child's self-concept and racial identity. However, these results and implications are questionable, if not quite fallacious. Many of these studies have been conducted with preschool children whose behaviors may not generalize to all Black children. Also, until the social antecedents to racial identity and self-concept formation are identified, this research has limited application.

The issue of language abilities in inner-city children has led to a heated controversy outweighed only by the issue of intelligence. Much of the research has measured language performance and inferred language competence. It has emphasized the inner-city child's comprehension of standard English while minimizing the importance of the child's production of Black English. Of course, there are exceptions (Labov 1973; Hall and Freedle 1975), but there has been very little recognition that inner-city children have a wide variety of language skills. Greater attention has been paid to whether the language of inner-city children represents either a different or deviant language system. The weight of evidence from both anthropological viewpoints and transformational linguistics demonstrates the inadequacy of the deficit theory.

A third area of concern has been the inner-city child's intelligence test performance. The standardized IQ test does not measure components of native intelligence but rather previous formal and informal learning experiences. IQ scores of minority inner-city children are lower than normative middle SES scores; however, the 10 to 15 point difference between these groups probably indicates that we are unable to measure and give inner-city children credit for their intellectual capabilities. Samuda (1975) has provided a potent argument to demonstrate the limitations of standardized intelligence testing for minority inner-city children.

It might be more meaningful to examine cognitive functioning in terms of socialization processes. There is some indication that inner-city children's socialization experiences foster a unique perceptual-conceptual organization. Some research studies on differential patterns of cognitive functioning among ethnic groups have found that Black children perform best on verbal abilities and spatial conceptualization.

Appropriate research procedures for all three of these areas would be to identify the environmental origins of behavior, specifically socialization and the role of extra-familial influences. For example, an all Black community may offer more positive conditions for developing components of positive racial identity but not for positive self-concept (Dill 1975). Measuring Black children's racial attitudes showed some surprising responses. The instrument consisted of drawings of two people who were identical except for skin color. Children were asked to select either the White or Black person after being read a short passage describing positive or negative traits. Responses varied, as expected, but when asked why they selected the Black person as having negative traits, most of the children said that the described negative behavior reminded them of someone they knew—someone who, of course, was Black. This seems to indicate that White people may have very little salience for children living in an all Black community.

Another pertinent issue is that we tend to ignore the developmental issues of Black children's self-concept performances. As indicated earlier, young Black children have been found to have relatively low self-concepts. However, Blacks tend to have positive self-concept scores (often higher than Whites) during the preadolescent and adolescent years. Coleman (1966) interpreted such results as indicative of unrealistic fantasylike behavior on the part of Black youths! The issue of self-concept must remain an open book until all dimensions have been thoroughly examined.

The issues of intelligence and linguistic performance among inner-city children are more complex. We need to completely abandon the practice of testing for intelligence until some of the basic theoretical and psychometric issues are resolved. Similarly, many controversies regarding language can be resolved by recognizing the functional equivalence of all language systems and by going beyond experimental procedures that simply examine comparative performance on standardized tests.

THE FOUNDATION FOR A DEVELOPMENTAL THEORY

My primary concern is to provide a foundation for the construction of a psychological theory of inner-city children's behavior. A theory is a set of concepts, definitions, and propositions that systematically specify the relationship among variables and has as its purpose explanation and prediction of the phenomena under investigation (Kerlinger 1973). The first two steps in the process—(1) exploring the relevant content areas, selecting major issues, and developing promising con-

cepts; and (2) defining and designating the relationships between concepts—have been taken in the preceding discussion. The next step is to adopt a developmental perspective so that the theory is concerned with changes in behavior that occur over time. These changes lead to alterations in the form and organization of behavior. Thus, for the inner-city child, we must ask: What are the transitional rules that govern change? What are the critical experiences that foster change? Does developmental change imply reversibility or irreversibility? We must then examine the role of such factors as mothering styles, the role of fathers and other family members, the mediating factors related to achievement motivation, and the antecedent conditions related to specific personality characteristics in the inner-city child.

The three major developmental orientations represented by psychoanalysis, social learning theory, and cognitive-developmental theory are somewhat useful in terms of inner-city children. Psychoanalysis, as a biological theory, has stimulated a great deal of interest in the early childhood years. Its focus on parent-child interactions has provided a conceptual framework for understanding dynamics of early human experiences. Does this mean that psychoanalysis has very circumscribed applications for inner-city children? I would think so except for understanding such things as the developmental patterns, ego defense mechanisms, the role of sex-role identity, and possibly the role of superego functions as related to the incorporation of moral standards.

Social learning theory offers more promise, with the advantage of interrelating theoretical issues with empirical findings. We are also able to rely on more realistic and tangible factors and conditions which determine inner-city children's behavioral development. For example, two key concepts from this theory, imitation and modeling, can provide critical understandings about the course of development and learning in inner-city children. We need to understand how children's imitative behaviors operate and determine sex-role identity, racial identity, motivation, and other behaviors. Modeling processes are similarly important, since this issue always arises in the case of father-absent inner-city males. My primary reservation with social learning theory, however, is its stress on the experimental method. We need a more enriching method to arrive at major issues applicable to inner-city children.

Cognitive-developmental theory as proposed by Piaget and his followers maintains that the basic mental structure is a product of interactional patterning between the organism and the environment. Unfortunately, many people have misinterpreted this theory by assuming that it stresses maturational processes while ignoring environmental influences. Others have constructed measuring techniques that emphasize individual differences rather than the origin and development of mental structures. Some have been overzealous in constructing curricular programs based on Piaget's theories. I suggest that a systematic analysis of the applicability of Piagetian theory to the behavior of inner-city children be considered. Much of Piaget's approach to the development of knowledge and thought would be quite meaningful in understanding the behavior of inner-city children.

In examining these major developmental theories, I have selected some of their cogent components for analysis and application to inner-city children's behavior. This critique is far from exhaustive. Yet, my general evaluation of these theories is that it is not very fruitful to apply a theory to a child or, conversely, to try and make the child's behavior fit the theory. Often this is how the inner-city child has been viewed by psychologists.

There is a need for constructing alternative theories and models of development for inner-city children. Although some might argue that theory construction is an intellectual extravagance that fails to address the immediate social and educational concerns for inner-city children, my position is that our present programmatic efforts have not succeeded partially because of the absence of a workable and effective theory.

In beginning to construct this developmental theory, three major issues will be addressed: the prerequisite rules (or metatheoretical components), the effective methodological approaches, and some preliminary constructs.

Prerequisite Rules

The metatheoretical aspects provide the proper orientation for the proposed theory and also indicate its soundness. Does the theory adequately apply to the majority of children under consideration? Is the theory comprehensive yet sensitive to basic social realities? Can the theory be modified to generate even more meaningful underpinnings of behavior? Perhaps the major metatheoretical aspect of this developmental theory is that it must be *ecologically valid*. A systematic examination of the environment must include an analysis of both functional and operational determinants. Second, we must understand how the continuity of environmental influences operates at different developmental periods. Some researchers have identified environmental process variables which indicate how the environment operates rather than using descriptions of the environment (Tulkin 1972). Thus, it may not be important if a child's father is an engineer or a janitor; more critical may be the nature of the interaction that the father has with the child.

A second metatheoretical issue is that the proposed developmental theory should be *positivistic*. The orientation should not focus on such issues as the dynamics of conflicts, the control of instinctual impulses, or the notion of pathological/deviant behavior. In contrast, there is a need to identify the origin and course of behavior and the variables which influence it. As an illustration, let us suppose that we are concerned with the development of perceptual-motor skills of inner-city infants. Instead of focusing on whether infant behaviors deviate from the norm, our concern should be with the appropriate experiences which will facilitate skill development in this area. The same approach could apply to language ability, racial identity, and cognitive performance.

The third metatheoretical issue would emphasize *intraindividualistic* rather than interindividualistic approaches. We would no longer focus on comparative indexes, especially between groups, but instead would stress the directionality and growth within the individual child. For example, we are concerned with attaining positive racial identity in inner-city children. The problem with such a goal is that it is too universal and does not account for the specific personality makeup of particular children. The intraindividualistic approach, however, would take into account the child's individuality and construct alternative patterns of fostering positive racial identity appropriate for a particular child. This intraindividualistic approach would also take into account the relative effectiveness of differential reward systems and experiences for a child.

Methodology

These three approaches suggest that a particular methodology should be considered. At the present time, much of our developmental research is centered around experimental procedures. This is not fortuitous since most developmental psychologists endorse the viewpoint that experimentation provides the only (or the best) systematic means of deriving sound theoretical concepts (Zigler 1963). However, initially we need to conduct systematic naturalistic observations of inner-city children's behavior. Then the careful use of experimental procedures should be implemented. Procedures such as those used in ethographic studies provide appropriate models (Jones 1972).

Emerging Theoretical Constructs

While the following theoretical constructs are incomplete, they are nevertheless heuristic. Each of these constructs is focused around a social matrix (social means that the interaction of the child with another person is highly significant; similarly, the concept of a matrix implies a

pattern, network, or setting). Combined, these terms refer to the constellation of critical life events occurring at various points on the developmental continuum. Within this constellation would be included such key elements as the child, family members, family interactional dynamics, and relevant environmental influences.

Prenatal-perinatal environmental matrix: Environmental influences beginning at conception and continuing through gestation can affect the child's subsequent behavioral growth and development. Inner-city children have a higher incidence of prenatal and perinatal complications that may very well influence their potentialities; such problems may originate during the preadolescent period of the child's mother (Birch and Gussow 1970). Thus, the overwhelming health-related problems that can influence so many inner-city children need to be addressed not only in theory development but also in terms of additional research and intervention efforts.

Mother-child matrix: Our present base of data about mother-infant relationships (attachment) has been enriching. However, application of this information to inner-city children might be limited unless specific consideration is given to cultural variables. In addition, the antecedents of this relationship, the role of other caregivers, and its stability and developmental course would provide major areas for study. Also, what role does institutional intervention play in either facilitating or inhibiting this relationship? I suspect that such intervention, unless it is fully understood by all participants, will do more damage in terms of the ultimate development of the child.

Immediate and global environmental matrix— *often called environmental process variables (Wolfe 1964):* The effects on the child of both direct and indirect influences by persons and institutions should be measured. For example, what do parents do to foster intellectual or personality development? What are the influences of the family status relative to various institutions? Many inner-city families are characterized by the intensity of family members' participation in various social organizations and networks. These experiences carry value systems and directed behaviors that may influence the child's behavior; nuances of such factors need to be examined.

Developmental continuum matrix: Although we generally consider the first five years as critical in terms of children's development, for inner-city children the first fifteen years are critical. Of course, specific areas of development would occur at different times. The first five years are certainly primary in terms of many aspects of cognitive development. Social and personality development take place over a longer time period. The transition from family-based to peer-group-based influences would provide us with a better understanding of specific aspects of personality development of inner-city children. Antecedents to a positive racial identity might be found to develop during the formative years while the child is under the influence of the family, but this might be reversed or modified by peers during preadolescence. Either deprivation or enrichment during early developmental experiences must be considered in examining subsequent experiences. Critical developmental experiences for inner-city children might well occur during adolescence, in contrast to earlier periods for the middle SES child. For many inner-city youths, there is a conflict between parental and peer group value systems.

An alternative theory of development for inner-city children should be formulated. The framework of such a theory could be constructed around the various metatheoretical constructs listed above. Various effective methodological approaches should be considered. Some of the basic constructs of the proposed developmental theory have been outlined. Although this theory of development is far from complete, it is a necessary beginning.

References

Allen, V. L. *Psychological Factors in Poverty*. Chicago: Markham, 1970.

Birch, H. G., and Gussow, J. D. *Disadvantaged Children: Health, Nutrition and School Failure*. New York: Grune & Stratton, 1970.

Clark, K. B., and Clark, M. P. "Skin Color as a Factor in the Racial Identification in Negro Preschool Children." *Journal of Social Psychology* 11 (1940): 159-169.

Coleman, J. S., et al. *Equality of Educational Opportunity*. Washington, D.C.: U.S. Department of Health, Education, and Welfare, 1966.

Dill, J. R. "Black Father-Son Interaction: Indices of Socialization." Paper presented at biennial meeting of the Society for Research in Child Development, 1975, Denver, Colo.

Hall, W. S., and Freedle, R. *Culture and Language: The Black American Experience*. New York: Halsted Press, 1975.

Hess, R. D. "Social Class and Ethnic Influences in Socialization." In *Carmichael's Manual of Child Psychology*, edited by P. H. Mussen. New York: John Wiley & Sons, 1970.

Jones, N. B., ed. *Ethological Studies of Child Behaviour*. London: Cambridge University Press, 1972.

Kerlinger, F. *Foundations of Behavioral Research: Educational, Psychological, and Sociological Inquiry*. 2nd ed. New York: Holt, Rinehart and Winston, 1973.

Labov, W. *Language in the Inner City: Studies in the Black English Vernacular*. Philadelphia: University of Pennsylvania Press, 1973.

Langer, J. *Theories of Development*. New York: Holt, Rinehart and Winston, 1969.

Leacock, E. B., ed. *The Culture of Poverty: A Critique*. New York: Simon and Schuster, 1971.

Porter, J. *Black Child, White Child: The Development of Racial Attitudes*. Cambridge, Mass.: Harvard University Press, 1971.

Samuda, R. J. *Psychological Testing of American Minorities*. New York: Dodd, Mead, 1975.

Silverstein, B., and Krate, R. *Children of the Dark Ghetto*. New York: Praeger, 1975.

Tulkin, S. "An Analysis of the Concept of Cultural Deprivation." *Developmental Psychology* 6 (1972): 326-339.

Wolfe, R. "The Measurement of Environments." In *Testing Problems in Perspective*, edited by A. Anastasi. Washington, D.C.: American Council on Education, 1965.

Zigler, E. F. "Metatheoretical Issues in Developmental Psychology." In *Theories in Contemporary Psychology*, edited by M. Marx. New York: Macmillan, 1963.

The Family Structure of Inner-City Children

Much has been written about the structure or the lack of structure of the inner-city family. Some findings suggest that low socioeconomic environments create different pathological behaviors in children. These pathological behaviors are usually attributed to the family who supposedly could not provide the children with the kind of environment they needed to develop appropriately.

We recognize that much of what parents do with their children either enhances or stifles the children's growth and development. If it is valid to believe that inner-city parents lack vital parenting behaviors, then inner-city children may continue to evidence a greater number of pathologies than their non-inner-city counterparts. Herein lies the problem. First, causal links between specific parenting behaviors and optimum development are undetermined.

Indeed, what is "optimum development"? The term demands a referent, such as school success or coping with present environmental demands. Whatever the referent, the gap in the literature remains. In addition, the impact of the settings chosen for data collection on parenting skills has largely been ignored. This has led to a criticism of the reliability and validity of differences identified. That is, it is impossible to ascertain whether socioeconomic status-race differences in parenting behaviors are generalizable to nonlaboratory situations. Further criticism of studies of inner-city family structures results from the focus of the research itself. Family structure, albeit a potentially powerful variable, is but one variable affecting child behavior. Descriptive studies of parenting behaviors in no way allow a research worker to infer that parenting behaviors are causally linked to child behaviors. We feel that the great emphasis placed upon family structure is well taken. However, research must concomitantly investigate other factors in a child's environment.

Phyllis Dukes presents a review of the literature on childrearing practices and the effects those practices have on the cognitive development of children. She argues that numerous studies examining the relationship between childrearing practices and their impact on cognitive development have used flawed methodologies. She further shows how these methodological flaws contributed to the myth that low-income parents are inadequate in their parenting practices. In conclusion, Dukes strongly advocates that future research should be ecological in nature, describing the interrelationships of a variety of variables in the inner-city child's environment. We add our recommendation for data collection in situ to increase the ecological validity of data obtained.

Pamela Reid reviews research conducted during the last fifteen years examining the effects of maternal dominance on Black children. Reid discusses the societal roles that are defined for males and females in this country. Moreover, she describes the value society places on the different roles. The characteristics of the matriarchy model as defined by social scientists are described and the limitations of that model are discussed.

These chapters are complementary in that they strongly suggest that educators and social scientists must begin viewing inner-city children and their families in their total environmental context.

Phyllis J. Dukes

The Effects of Early Childrearing Practices on the Cognitive Development of Infants

Research on childrearing, infant care practices, and parental value systems has been the focus of sociological and psychological studies for the past twenty years. Beginning with the Havighurst and Davis study (1955), most of the studies have attempted to establish differences in childrearing practices by the socioeconomic status (SES) of parents. From the reports of this research and their subsequent incorporation into the literature, there has emerged considerable consensus concerning changing childrearing patterns and certain SES-associated differences in these goals, techniques, and value systems (Bronfenbrenner 1961; Kohn 1959; Miller and Swanson 1959; Reissman 1959).

The emphasis of many of the studies has shifted away from studies of SES and childrearing personality to SES and cognitive studies, with particular focus on mother-child interactions. The assumptions of the latter studies appeared to be that the early experiences which are part of mother-child interactions shape thought and cognitive styles of problem solving. The problem with many of these studies is that they rest on the assumption that "differences" in childrearing methods of poor and minority groups lead to "deficits" in children's intellectual skills. Thus poor children's environment is automatically assumed to affect their cognitive performance. The overriding theme in most of the studies reviewed is that middle SES childrearing methods are a model of effective parenting which leads to greater cognitive gains. The consequence of using these earlier assumptions as theoretical bases has led to the support of SES differentiated value systems in childrearing. Numerous questions have been raised concerning the methods employed in these studies, and the authors themselves have carefully qualified their results. Yet, the conclusions have been incorporated into the childrearing literature and have been used as bases for further research, for interpretations of related data, and for speculation concerning effects upon American children.

Beginning with the Coleman Report (1966) which showed that poor children do less well than their middle SES counterparts in school, and using the Moynihan Report (1965) as evidence to why these children do so poorly, investigators began to focus their attention on the parents, particularly the mother, as the prime factor in promoting intellectual competence. Because middle SES children consistently scored higher on tests measuring cognitive performance, it was assumed that whatever childrearing methods the middle SES mother was using, they were supportive of intellectual competence.

Since the schools, and particularly the Head Start classes, were unable to "make up" for the "deficits" in the poor child's learning capacity, and supported by proof from Bloom (1964) that 80 percent of the child's intellect was acquired by age three, psychologists turned their attention to the period of infancy. Although there was very little empirical data which linked infants' abilities below age three to any correlational outcomes of intellectual achievement during school age, numerous investigators began looking for infant cognitive differences among different socioeconomic groups (Bayley 1965; Golden and Birns 1968; Knobloch and Pasamanick 1960). When such factors as birth complications, poor nutrition, and health were ruled out, none of these studies found infant cognitive differences among different SES groups during the first two years of life.

What are the implications of these studies in terms of the effects of parent-child interactions on infant development? Although the interest of the studies was sociologically and psychologically sound, the indexes used assumed that an association between infant care practices, values of the parents, and cognitive development of children had already been substantiated. In reviewing the findings from some of the major childrearing studies (Davis and Havighurst 1946; Kohn 1959; Littman et al. 1957; Maccoby and Gibbs 1954), many conflicting results were found. Because the previous studies conducted focused on the American culture, using the White middle SES value system as a standard of measurement for effective parenting, the myth of the low SES inadequacies in childrearing practices emerged, with particular implications for Black parents, who were the focus of most of the studies.

It appeared to me that what many of my fellow researchers had neglected was cross-cultural validation of their theories and a more ecological system of analyses.

Cultural differences among groups have been the most frequently used model of comparison in the socialization literature (Barry, Bacon, and Child 1957; Cole 1971; Greenfield and Bruner 1969; Mead 1928; Whiting 1963). Very few psychologists, however, have attempted to examine the family socialization processes on a more anthropological basis. The anthropologists for years have used the ecological model in studying group differences (Gay and Cole 1967; LeVine and LeVine 1963; Whiting and Child 1953). Instead of merely observing different outcome behaviors, the anthropologist is more interested in the conditions of the external social and cultural world in which the child lives, the adaptive consequences which the adults in the environment acquire in their interactions with this system, in what specific forms adult orientations appear in interaction with children, and with the behavioral outcomes of these experiences (Hess 1970). Using this method, a linkage is drawn between the society, its institutions, conditions of life, and the behavior of adults who act as socializing agents for their children. Thus, the emphasis is placed on studying the child in relationship to his or her own particular social and cultural setting.

I would like to discuss some of the ecological variables of socialization that affect young children's development and that have been most neglected in Western European research. The work of Whiting and Whiting (1959) will be relied upon heavily as a model.

HOUSEHOLD COMPOSITION

The number of socializing agents in a family contributes to different childrearing techniques. Since the mother and father have been viewed as the primary socializing agents, it was assumed by several investigators (Bowlby 1951; Casler 1961; Spitz 1945) that the lack of one parent or both causes serious cognitive and affective deficits in the child. Multiple mothering, or a variety of caregivers, was also considered detrimental to the young child (Goldfarb 1945). Several investigators (Cole et al. 1971; Murdock 1957; Munroe and Munroe 1975; Whiting et al. 1966) have shown, however, that in comparison with households cross-culturally, only about one quarter of the world's cultures utilize the nuclear family model.

The amount and quality of the child's interactions with socializing agents may differ substantially depending on whether a child is raised in a nuclear family model or a more social type of living arrangement. For example, Whiting found the number of people in the household affects the timing and techniques of socialization. She discovered weaning and independence training are usually begun earlier in a nuclear family, because of the competitive need of the mother by both the father and the child.

Age and severity of aggression training and the techniques parents employ are also affected by household composition. Murdock (1957) found children's aggression is most severely prohibited in societies with extended households. The social development of the child is also affected by the number of people available for the child to identify with, imitate, or internalize their values.

Another consideration of household composition is the child's sleeping arrangements. It is a common practice in many non-European societies (Rajputs of India, Japanese in Okinawa) for infants to sleep in the same bed with their parents, particularly the mother, before the child is weaned (Whiting 1963). In many societies (Mexitecans of Mexico, Trobrianders of New Guinea), the sleeping arrangement of the child is used for transition from one maturational stage to another (Munroe and Munroe 1975). The sleeping patterns of these societies are seen as an important variable in the attachment of the child to a specific sex-role model.

STATUS IN HOUSEHOLD

Very closely associated with household composition for many cultures is one's status in the household. This status may not be based on economics but on the importance placed on certain individuals within a family or community. For example, grandparents in the Ainu culture of Japan have a high role status in child training. In New Guinea, the male child is very close to the father in his early years, but after age six, authority for this training is turned over to his maternal uncle (Munroe and Munroe 1975). Within the family structure, the young child internalizes the prestige attached to various members within the group and quickly learns to respect prestigious group members, to fear certain family members, and to seek security and affection from still others. The particular role value as-

signed to the persons the child interacts most with can affect the child's cognitive and social behavior.

COMMUNITY SETTING

The density of the neighborhood and the type of households in a given community determine the mobility of the child, the resources available to the child, and the child's leisure activities. Contingent upon each of these variables is the type and quality of learning experiences to which the child will be exposed.

In the Gusiian community of Kenya, children are largely restricted in the range of their friendships and associations. Unless the family owns a herd of cattle, children are expected to stay close to home (Munroe and Munroe 1975). Within our own culture, we can see differences among communities in terms of the neighborhood setting. For example, in a suburban community the child will more than likely have a large yard to play in; plenty of trees; grass and space surrounding the house; large well-equipped play areas; quiet, traffic-free streets; and large well-equipped shopping centers. Residents of the community are usually friendly but somewhat reserved. In contrast, a young child growing up in a poor urban ghetto would be surrounded by crowded apartments; small houses, grouped close together; or projects where residents share a common play area, wash area, etc. Usually the streets of a poor community are used for socializing. In place of trees and large grassy areas, there are numerous storefront churches, neighborhood stores, bars, and litter. Because of lack of space, the residents communicate daily, share common experiences, and comprise a sort of extended family network. A child born in an urban poor area has a completely different set of experiences and social contacts.

The childrearing techniques used by parents have to be consistent with the demands of their particular community setting in an attempt to equip their children with the needed tools for adapting to their environment. Thus the emphases of childrearing would be quite different for a middle SES parent and a lower-income parent. The same would hold true for parents of rural communities.

CLIMATE AND GEOGRAPHIC LOCATION

Geographic location and climate affect the type of activities the family can engage in—the form of clothing worn (whether restrictive or loosely fitting), the amount of outdoor physical play allowed the child, the health and physical well being of the community residents, and the adaptive survival techniques utilized. Each of these aspects of environment greatly affects the socialization values and methods used by parents in childrearing.

ECONOMIC BASE

The economic base of a given group is directly related to the ecology of its surroundings. It is well known that the family's income is a major variable in determining one's economic base. However, there are other important aspects of one's economic base that are often overlooked, such as the material resources available in the home, availability of community goods and services, occupational demands, spacing of children, medical and nutritional resources. The amount and quality of material resources available to various groups for supporting a family is very important.

If the economy of the group is dependent on materials that must be purchased, then the income of the family greatly affects what the mother can provide for her child. In those groups dependent upon supplying their own goods by direct labor such as farming, fishing, sewing, or pottery, the economic demands of the family will determine the type of child training that receives first priority and the types of skill training the children will receive. For example, the sea is the main source of food for the Ainu of Japan; therefore, their homes are located along the river. By the age of five or six, boys are taught how to ride in a boat and help their fathers on fishing trips, and girls are taught domestic duties (Munroe and Munroe 1975).

In a more industrialized society, the types of jobs available to various members of a group, particularly the father, will affect the type of socialization pattern the father uses with his children. White collar workers are more inclined to stress intellectual competence, competitiveness, and a motivation to succeed in the academic or business world. A blue collar worker may emphasize more independence, flexibility, manual dexterity, aggressiveness, and athletic involvement.

The spacing of children in many societies is based upon the economics of the family. Children are either used to supplement the family income (Mexitecans of Mexico)—in which case bearing many children is considered a family asset—or children are carefully planned and controlled by weaning patterns or sexual taboos (Rajputs of India).

The availability of medical and nutritional resources is dependent upon the family economics. Studies have been conducted, both within our culture and cross-culturally, regarding the effects of medical and nutritional deficiencies on learning in infancy. Investigators in this area believe malnutrition and inadequate medical attention retard the appearance of specific developmental stages. In early infancy visual attentiveness may be lowered by malnutrition, and in later infancy it may depress the exploratory behavior of the child as well as lower alertness and attentiveness. Because health and nutritional variables often interact, it is difficult to determine whether inadequate nutrition leads directly to poor physical health, or other factors associated with poverty contribute directly to an unhealthy child.

CONCLUSIONS AND SUMMARY

After reviewing some of the ecological variables that contribute to differences in childrearing, it becomes even more obvious that many of the past researchers (in their haste to identify "deficits" in the lower-income family structure) as an explanation of "differences" in resulting child behaviors, have relied completely upon bias measures with total disregard for differences in conditions and circumstances surrounding the life-style of the children. One of the major premises posited by Cole and Bruner (1971) is "one of the most important things about any underlying competence is the nature of the situation in which it expresses itself" (p. 874).

In reviewing the changes in childrearing practices through the various time spans (Walters and Crandall 1964; Dittmann 1968), it appears that proper childrearing procedures are dictated by the behavioral science group most popular for the era. Since middle SES mothers follow the advice of "childrearing experts," their childrearing methods are likely to change tremendously from one period of time to another. Thus, we have seen the change from restrictive to permissive measures from 1940 to 1950 and a reversal in 1960 back to more restrictive measures.

Now, in the 1970s, the developmentalists (i.e., Piaget) are in control, and parents are more concerned with facilitating age-appropriate behaviors in their children. Because the working class parents cannot afford the luxury of changing childrearing methods every ten years to keep up with the popular view of the time, they tend to rely on methods that have been found effective in the past and that have been handed down through generations. Even if some of the techniques used are not always the most suitable for the child, at least there is some level of consistency that the child soon learns to identify and expect.

In considering how these various childrearing methods affect the thinking processes of young children, it is still unclear in the socialization literature how these two variables interact. It has been established in the child development literature, particularly for infants, that certain cognitive skills such as perception, language, and object concept have their emergence in infancy, and that these skills lead to more complex future behaviors. Thus, the infants' experiences play a major role in the rate of the emergence of these skills. What has not been established, however, particularly based on evidence from cross-cultural research, is whether or not the *rate* of emergence has any effect on the *quality* of the final outcome.

In conclusion, it appears that the myth of inadequate and ineffective parent-child interactions in low-income families is one that has been perpetrated by middle SES psychologists and educators who have rendered cultural and socioeconomic status differences of the poor and minority groups into deficits based upon the American middle SES yardstick of success.

References

Barry, L.; Bacon, M.; and Child, O. "A Class-Cultural Survey of Sex Differences and Socialization." *Journal of Abnormal and Social Psychology* 55, no. 3 (1957).

Bayley, N. "Comparisons of Mental and Motor Test Scores for Ages 1-15 Months by Sex, Birth Order, Race, Geographical Location and Education of Parents." *Child Development* 36 (1965): 370-411.

Bloom, B. S. *Stability and Change in Human Characteristics.* New York: John Wiley & Sons, 1964.

Bowlby, J. *Maternal Care and Mental Health.* Monograph 2. Geneva, Switzerland: World Health Organization, 1951.

Bronfenbrenner, U. "Toward a Theoretical Model for the Analysis of Parent-Child Relationships in a Social Context." In *Parental Attitudes and Child Behavior,* edited by J. C. Glidewell, pp. 19-109. Springfield, Ill.: Charles C. Thomas, 1961.

Casler, L. "Maternal Deprivation: A Critical Review of the Literature." *Monographs of the Society for Research in Child Development* 26, no. 2, Serial No. 80 (1961).

Cole, M., and Bruner, J. S. "Cultural Differences and Inferences about Psychological Processes." *American Psychologist* (1971): 867-876.

Cole, M.; Gay, J.; Glick, J.; and Sharp, D. W. *The Cultural Context of Learning and Thinking.* New York: Basic Books, 1971.

Coleman, J. S., with Campbell, E. Q.; Hobson, C. J.; et al. "Equality of Educational Opportunity." Washington, D.C.: U.S. Government Printing Office, 1966.

Davis, A., and Havighurst, R. J. "Social Class and Color Differences in Child Rearing." *American Sociological Review* 11 (1946): 698-710.

Dittmann, L. L., ed. *Early Child Care: The New Perspectives.* Chicago: Aldine Publishing Co., 1968.

Gay, J., and Cole, M. *The New Mathematics and an Old Culture.* New York: Holt, Rinehart and Winston, 1967.

Golden, M., and Birns, B. "Social Class and Cognitive Development in Infancy." *Merrill-Palmer Quarterly* 14 (1968): 139-149.

Goldfarb, W. "Psychological Privation in Infancy and Subsequent Adjustment." *American Journal of Orthopsychiatry* 15 (1945): 247-255.

Greenfield, P. M., and Bruner, J. S. "Culture and Cognitive Growth." In *Socialization Theory and Research,* edited by D. A. Goslin, pp. 633-657. Chicago: Rand McNally College Publishing Co., 1969.

Havighurst, R. J., and Davis, A. "A Comparison of the Chicago and Harvard Studies of Social Class Differences in Child Rearing." *American Sociological Review* 20 (1955): 438-442.

Hess, R. D. "The Transmission of Cognitive Strategies in Poor Families: The Socialization of Apathy and Underachievement." In *Psychological Factors in Poverty,* edited by V. L. Allen, pp. 74-92. Chicago: Markham Publishing Co., 1970.

Kohn, M. L. "Social Class and Parental Values." *American Journal of Sociology* 64 (1959): 337-351.

Knobloch, H., and Pasamanick, B. "Environmental Factors Affecting Human Development Before and After Birth." *Pediatrics* 26 (1960): 210-218.

LeVine, R. A., and LeVine, B. B. "Nyansongo: A Gusii Community in Kenya." In *Six Cultures: Studies of Child Rearing,* edited by B. B. Whiting. New York: John Wiley & Sons, 1963.

Littman, R. A.; Moore, R. A.; and Pierce-Jones, J. "Social Class Differences in Child Rearing: A Third Community for Comparison with Chicago and Newton." *American Sociological Review* 22 (1957): 694-704.

Maccoby, E., and Gibbs, P. K. "Methods of Childrearing in Two Social Classes." In *Readings in Child Development,* edited by W. E. Martin and C. B. Stendler, pp. 380-396. New York: Harcourt Brace, 1954.

Mead, M. *Coming of Age in Samoa.* New York: William Morrow, 1928.

Miller, D. R., and Swanson, G. E. *Inner Conflict and Defense.* New York: Holt, Rinehart and Winston, 1960.

Moynihan, D. P. *The Negro Family: The Case for National Action.* Washington, D.C.: U.S. Department of Labor, U.S. Government Printing Office, 1965.

Murdock, G. P. "Anthropology as a Comparative Science." *Behavioral Science* 2 (1957): 249-254.

Munroe, R. L., and Munroe, R. H. *Cross-Cultural Human Development.* Monterey, Calif.: Brooks/Cole Publishing Co., 1975.

Reissman, L. *Class in American Society.* Glencoe, Ill.: Free Press, 1959.

Spitz, R. A. "Hospitalism: An Inquiry into the Genesis of Psychiatric Conditions in Early Childhood, I." *The Psychoanalytic Study of the Child* 1 (1945): 53-74.

Walters, E., and Crandall, V. J. "Social Class and Observed Maternal Behavior from 1940-1960." *Child Development* 35 (1964): 1021-1032.

Whiting, B. B., ed. *Six Cultures: Studies of Child Rearing.* New York: John Wiley & Sons, 1963.

Whiting, J. W. M., and Child, I. L. *Child Training and Personality.* New Haven, Conn.: Yale University Press, 1953.

Whiting, J. W. M.; Child, I. L.; Lambert, W. W.; et al. *Field Guide for Study of Socialization.* New York: John Wiley & Sons, 1966.

Whiting, J. W. M., and Whiting, B. B. "Contributions of Anthropology to Methods of Studying Child Rearing." In *Handbook of Research Methods in Child Development,* edited by P. H. Mussen. New York: John Wiley & Sons, 1959.

Pamela Trotman Reid

Are Black Children Feminized by Maternal Dominance?

Research conducted during the past fifteen years in the area of sex-role development suggests that Black children deviate from the norms defined by society. The primary explanation offered for the deviation is that Black families do not fit the pattern of the typical White American family; the Black American family is dominated by the mother. In this chapter a review of the literature is presented in an attempt to determine, first, whether dominance patterns of Black and White families do differ, and secondly, to what extent do familial dominance patterns, or parental characteristics, affect the sex-role development of children. It is hypothesized that there are no qualitative differences in familial dominance between Blacks and Whites, but that differences are merely a matter of degree. It is also suggested that familial characteristics do influence the development of sex-role behavior but that it would be difficult to establish a direct relationship between that behavior and any specific characteristic because the relationship is so complex.

TRADITIONAL SEX-ROLE MODEL

In American society a clear and recognizable distinction exists between the masculine and the feminine roles (Joshi 1970). A survey of adult men and women revealed a surprising degree of agreement on these sex-role stereotypes (Holter 1970). Men were considered dominant, aggressive, independent, and unemotional; women were described as more subordinate, gentle, sociable, less self-confident, and emotional. Elkin and Handel (1972) recognized that these sex-role expectations are not fully determined by anatomy or by the purely biological determinants of behavior. Societal training contributes heavily to the expectations and definitions of these roles. Not only have separate behavior patterns been defined for males and females, but a difference in the degree of importance of the two roles has been ascribed. Greater status, moreover, is accorded to the male role at all levels of society and by both sexes (Connell and Johnson 1970). Both male and female college students placed a higher value on stereotypic masculine characteristics than on feminine characteristics (Rosenkrantz, Vogel, Bee, Broverman, and Broverman 1968). Experiments which offer children a choice between sex-appropriate and inappropriate toys indicate that the preferential status of male playthings is recognized early in life (Munger 1971).

There is a tendency, beginning in childhood and continuing through adulthood, for children to devalue feminine characteristics. Baruch (1972) suggests that these standards are learned from the mother. Since little value is placed on homemaking by women or by society, negative attitudes are developed in children toward that behavior, while positive attitudes toward the more highly valued masculine behavior are fostered. The subordinate role held by females in the home and the dominant role maintained by men is also presented to children and perpetuated by television programming (Sternglanz and Serbin 1974).

Since psychological well being within our society is, to an important degree, related to the individual's acceptance of appropriate sex-role, it is disturbing when it is suggested that an entire segment of the population does not conform to the accepted role. This is what has occurred in the case of Black children as interpreted by researchers.

MATRIARCHY MODEL

The model of the Black family has been defined by sociologists, psychologists, and other social scientists as being different from that of the average White family with respect to values and sex-role behavior. In the White family, the man has the dominant role and is expected to support and lead the family. In Black ghetto life, Black men are considered to be unwilling to accept domestic responsibilities. According to Rainwater (1966), Black boys learn that the safest role for young men to adopt is that of lover, because the role of father and provider too easily leads to failure. Hannerz (1969) also presented a negative image of the Black man as a big talker but incapable of holding the dominant position in the home. Black girls, on the other hand, are the ones who learn to manage the family affairs, and, as women, they dominate the men. While White women have the subservient role and are described as presenting a weak and passive image to their children, Black women have been described as having the opposite effect on their children.

Traditionally, Black females have surpassed males in academic achievement and have attained higher educational status (Broom and Glenn 1965). More Black women work than do White women, and researchers lead us to believe that Black women are in a more stable economic position than are Black men (Hannerz 1969; Moynihan 1965). Moynihan (1965) has reported that one out of every four Black households is headed by a woman. Based on these statements researchers have concluded that dominance in the Black family belongs to women and that Black men do not have the power and superior status of White men in the home. The Black family has, therefore, been examined and interviewed to determine the effects of this social structure in which women have the dominant role.

The belief that a matriarchy exists has been supported by the number of Black women without husbands. The Moynihan report (1965) cited evidence that between 24 and 47 percent of low socioeconomic status Blacks were separated or divorced. In fact, father absence was identified as the most critical problem of the Black family by Moynihan. Subsequent studies of Black children and families characterized them as "father absent." The assumption was that due to the separation of Black fathers from their families, the children of those families lacked male models and reinforcement for masculine behavior. Miller (1958) presented a psychoanalytic rationale to explain the effects of father absence on boys' sex-role development. The young boy is believed to develop an excessively close identification with his mother, which later leads to denial of feminine traits and reaction formation (i.e., overassertion of masculine traits).

Although little evidence is presented in support of this hypothesis for American children, the data do seem to indicate that father absence disrupts the sex-role development of boys (Hetherington and Deur 1971). In a study of sex-role preference, Black boys made significantly more feminine choices than White boys when semiprojective instructions were given (Thompson and McCandless 1970). This outcome was interpreted as an indication that Black boys were exposed to weak male models in their environment and that the feminine role was preferred. Black girls in this study seemed to perceive the *it* figure as feminine more often than White girls, leading the researchers to again conclude that the female model in the Black family was seen as dominant and active.

ARGUMENTS AGAINST MATRIARCHY MODEL

When the research is carefully examined, the actual existence of a Black matriarchy becomes doubtful. TenHouten (1970) found that although

Black mothers tend to dominate in certain areas of family life, low socioeconomic status Blacks subscribed more strongly than Whites to the belief that males should dominate. King (1967) interviewed Black adolescents and produced no evidence to suggest that their family power structure was matriarchic. Using questionnaires and interaction situations, Mack (1971) found that there were no significant racial factors influencing the power structure in families, although there was a socioeconomic status difference. She concluded that working class husbands were slightly more powerful than their middle socioeconomic status counterparts in both Black and White families. With respect to economic dominance, Hill (1972) points out "that wives in poor black families contribute less to the total family income than do wives in non-poor black families because they are much less likely to be employed" (p. 13). From data presented in a 1970 population survey, Hill discovered that the total number of wives working was 20 percent less than the total number of husbands working. In addition, Black women earned significantly less than Black men, just as White women earned less than White men.

Although the majority of Black families are headed by the father, justifiable concern is directed toward those children who do not live with their fathers. Biller (1971) and Hetherington (1972; 1973) support the contention that fathers play an important role in the sex-role development of their daughters. They compared adolescent girls from father-absent families with girls from father-present families. It was found that girls without fathers, due to separation, divorce, or death exhibited inappropriate behavior in the presence of male examiners. The researchers suggested that girls without fathers are less likely to have satisfying heterosexual relationships. Hetherington also discovered, however, that there were no differences in the feminine interests or attitudes toward the feminine role among the groups of girls.

Are Black children actually lacking in male models? In his report of life in a low socioeco-

nomic status Black ghetto, Hannerz (1969) observed that many Black male models do exist for the children, even in the absence of their fathers. In many instances, the mother shares her home with a brother or another male relative; male friends may visit and influence the lives of children; neighborhood men, often highly visible, provide another source of male models. Clergymen, teachers, and community workers may also be available to act as models. In a study of working class and middle socioeconomic status Black families, Scanzoni (1971) found that 55 percent of the respondents had encountered an extrafamilial person who influenced them when they were teenagers. Finally, the role that television characters play as models in the development of attitudes and behavior in children has yet to be fully explored, but imitation of these characters is clearly present.

It can be seen, then, that fathers are not the only influence on sex-role development. In fact, mothers are found to play an influential role in the development of sex-appropriate behavior. Maternal encouragement and reward for masculine sex-role preferences and for masculine sex-role adoption are related to high self-image and masculinity in boys (Biller 1969; Kogan and Wimberger 1969). Discouragement by mothers of participation in masculine activities, and the reinforcement of feminine behaviors has been found to be related to feminine sex-role orientation and homosexuality in boys (Bieber et al. 1962; Harrington 1970; West 1967).

Results from studies concerning maternal influences on daughters have been the most equivocal. A positive relationship was found between girls' femininity and their mothers' control and nurturance by some researchers (Doherty 1970; Mussen and Rutherford 1963). Biller and Zung (1972), however, found that maternal control was indirectly related to the degree of masculine sex-role preference. Hetherington (1965) discovered that maternal dominance did not produce feminine sex-role preferences in girls. On the other hand, Rutherford (1965) concluded that feminine sex-role preference of young girls is influenced by the mothers' dominance and mastery in the home. Ward (1973) later hypothesized that girls do not consistently imitate their mothers, instead they seem to identify with a culturally-defined feminine role.

ALTERNATIVE BLACK SEX-ROLE MODEL

The fact that Black women hold a higher position in the family than do White women is generally accepted. The relevant questions are, "Do Black women dominate their families?" and "Do Black women keep Black men in the subordinate position?" As interpreted by many social researchers, the answer is that Black males do hold a less powerful position in Black society than do females. If, however, the fallacies leading to this conclusion are rejected, an alternative model must be considered. The interpretation proposed in this chapter is that Black society holds women in higher regard than does White society, but that dominance is maintained by men.

The implication of the proposed model for the behavior of Black children with respect to sex-role preferences is somewhat predictable. It is hypothesized that Black boys will not reject the feminine role to the extent that White boys will. However, they will prefer the masculine role and make more masculine choices than girls. Similarly, it is suggested that Black girls will accept the feminine role and make more feminine choices than will White girls. The greater acceptance of their feminine role combined with higher status for that role should result in Black girls having higher self-esteem than White girls. It is likely that the definitions of masculine and feminine in the Black family are broader and more inclusive than the traditionally accepted role definitions in White families.

It seems reasonable to suggest that this model of an egalitarian Black family offers a parsimonious explanation of much of the existing data. The greater respect and higher role status accorded Black females should not be interpreted as having an emasculating effect on Black males. The deleterious effects of unhappy or broken homes, of poverty, or of unstimulating environments cannot be ignored; however, the suggestion that the acceptance of feminine activities as worthy for males is maladaptive behavior perpetuates a stereotype that many in society are beginning to reject. In light of the recent emphasis on women's liberation, it could instead be suggested that Black children are especially adaptable and flexible in their roles. Black children do not seem to have the tendency to see "maleness" in all important or valuable activities.

Reexamining the Thompson and McCandless study, which was previously discussed, from this new perspective, the results are consistent. Black boys score higher in sex-role preference than Black and White girls in every condition. They did not choose more masculine toys than White boys, however, because they had a higher acceptance of feminine alternatives. Black girls also chose more feminine items than White girls, again, because the female role was viewed by them as a worthy one.

It remains clear, however, that more research should be conducted to explicate the factors influencing the sex-role development of Black children. Studies should attempt to define the masculine and feminine roles as they operate in Black society without injecting unfounded stereotypes. Comparisons must be judiciously studied to determine if the groups are indeed comparable on relevant independent variables. Finally, research dealing with the concepts of masculinity and femininity should abandon the assumption that they are dichotomous. Researchers may then begin to study the concepts "masculine" and "feminine" as distinct behavior patterns that can be simultaneously developed and measured. This will be forthcoming as attitudes toward feminine behavior become more positive.

CONCLUSIONS

In the final analysis, the answer to the question, "Are Black children feminized by maternal dominance?" depends on the interpretation of from their points of view. For the MRT, reviewers were selected from the following groups: Northern Urban Black, Northern Urban White, Southern Urban Black, Southern Urban White, Appalachian, Southwest American Indian, Chicano, Puerto Rican, and Cuban. Changes were made in the test based upon these reviews.

PRACTICE MATERIAL

Practice materials orienting the child to the test and reviewing specific skills and vocabulary help all children to succeed with the testing task. Practice material might include such skills as: turning and folding pages; concepts of row, shade box, page, next, top; the marking systems; page and row finders; and the item formats used in the test. The practice material teaches test-taking skills by using activities, ditto sheets, games, and practice tests. The MRT practice booklet may be used as often as necessary until each child is able to complete it with success. In no case should the readiness test be given to a child who has not mastered the practice activities. In addition, sample items for each subtest reviewing the specific item format and vocabulary help to make the test a fairer measure of skill development for all children.

TEST LEVELS

First grade children who have not been to kindergarten, who have poorly developed language skills, who have low socioeconomic level or limited experience backgrounds should be tested with a lower level test if possible, using grade one norms on a kindergarten test. This practice avoids giving children a frustrating failure experience and is less likely to produce an incorrect low score that might be used to label the child erroneously or misplace a child in a "slow" group. An informal reading test may be given to children who score high on the grade one test to determine if they are actually reading, thus avoiding unnecessary instruction in prereading skills. Grade one norms are provided for level I of the MRT (kindergarten level test).

SCORES

Reporting stanine scores for skill areas such as auditory skills, visual skills, or language skills allows broad interpretation and reduces the danger of overinterpretation of small, unreliable score differences. The MRT was developed to give the greatest spread of scores at the middle and low score ranges, thus maximizing the instructional information available to teachers.

Supplementary materials such as parent reports, observation checklists, and activity books assist the teachers in using a readiness test effectively. The goal is to provide as much instructional information from the test results as possible.

The key to testing having a positive, rather than negative, effect on inner-city children is the positive attitude of the teacher. Teachers who accept all children are open to each child's strengths and do not allow themselves to be misled by erroneous test results. The following checklist includes standards against which any test for young children should be examined and reviewed. These requirements should be added to the usual requirements of validity and reliability expected in any standardized test.

Checklist for Evaluating Readiness Tests for Young Children

1. Is the test content related to an analysis of skills?
2. Does the test measure instructional skills rather than aptitude?
3. Is it a measure of skills, not memory?
4. Are the illustrations familiar to children from all ethnic groups, sexes, socioeconomic levels, geographic areas?
5. Is the vocabulary familiar to all children?
6. Have items not found in some dialects or languages been omitted?
7. Was the test reviewed by professionals and parents representing various ethnic groups?
8. Did the standardization sample include a proportionate number of children of vari-

ous races, sexes, ethnic groups, socioeconomic levels, geographical areas, and community sizes?

9. Was a statistical test of internal item bias used?
10. Is adequate practice material included?
11. Do the scores provide clear, instructional information at all levels of development?
12. Are supplementary assessment and instructional materials provided?

References

Durkin, D. *Teaching Young Children to Read.* 2nd ed. Boston: Allyn and Bacon, 1976.

Nurss, J. R., and McGauvran, M. E. *The Metropolitan Readiness Tests Assessment Program.* New York: Harcourt Brace Jovanovich, 1976.

Scheuneman, J. "A New Method of Assessing Bias in Test Items." Paper presented at the meeting of the American Educational Research Association, April 1975, Washington, D.C.

Teachers and Inner-City Children

Research findings have consistently identified the teacher as a significant variable in educational programs. Perhaps most striking is the literature documenting that distinct populations of children within the same classroom continually have significantly different interactions with the same teacher. This literature in particular has focused on the different types of interactions that low- and high-achieving children have. It is generally accepted that a person's attitudes and beliefs are reliably evidenced in his or her behavior. Therefore, certain authors have argued that the changing of attitudes is a prerequisite to changing behavior. Certainly it is also possible that behavior change can lead to attitude change. Rather than examine the intricacies of that debate, we feel that either strategy, if employed in teacher training programs, may

lead to increasingly positive teacher attitudes and behavior. We recognize that attitude or behavior change still begs the question of how teacher behaviors are causally related to child performance. However, efforts to make teacher attitudes and beliefs less ethnocentric and stereotypic are in themselves eminently worthy. We feel the importance of the first two chapters in this section lies in their illustrations of specific procedures for the creation of positive attitudes in in-service teacher populations.

Ellen Jacobs and Jeffrey Derevensky report a study designed to make teacher perceptions of the inner-city environment more consonant with the perceptions of that environment held by inner-city children. They document, prior to treatment, that teachers with minimal exposure to the inner-city environment tend to view the inner city exclusively in terms of extreme poverty, deprivation, degradation, despair, and gloom. Conversely, teachers with more contact with the inner city understand its strengths as well as its weaknesses. Through a combination of teacher interviews with inner-city children, inner-city field placements, and observational assignments, Jacobs and Derevensky document one approach to making teacher perceptions of the inner city less narrow and stereotypic.

The form and function of the language of inner-city children who speak Black English has been a widely debated topic in early childhood education during the last decade. It has been well documented that teachers hold negative attitudes toward Black English. While the presence of negative attitudes is acknowledged, attempts to change those attitudes are just beginning to appear in the professional literature. Charles Billiard, Joan Elifson, and John Rubadeau discuss four studies designed to change the attitudes of teachers toward speech patterns that differ from standard English. The studies differ most importantly in their designs and methodologies. For example, one study emphasized the use of fieldwork in dialectology while other studies emphasized more "cognitive" treatments designed to effect attitude change through increased teacher information. The gratifying result was that the different methods each achieved positive results.

While many persons speak about basing educational experiences in the context of a child's culture, we have seen few attempts to do so described. Michele Rubin discusses her work as a teacher who implemented just such an attempt. In a refreshingly candid and readable account, Rubin describes her work with Black inner-city children and illustrates from that example a process for capitalizing on the cultural strengths of any group of children. We feel that this chapter provides clear support for the efficacy of working with children from a position of cultural strength rather than cultural deficit.

Ellen G. Jacobs and
Jeffrey L. Derevensky

Changing Teachers' Perceptions: A Look at the Inner-City Child's Environment

In recent years, investigators have begun to focus attention upon teacher values, attitudes, and belief systems and the effects of preconceived expectations on inner-city children (Becker 1952; Corwin and Schmit 1970; Miller and Woock 1973; Rist 1970; Rosenthal and Jacobson 1968).

The value systems for people of every social strata tend to be based on personal experiences. It has been proposed that teacher values and attitudes are the product of the teacher's social status. In addition, these values positively influence the teacher's attitudes toward children who most closely approximate these values (Rist 1970).

A substantial number of teachers working in the inner-city schools have been found to possess negative attitudes toward their pupils and would rather be in a different type of school (Becker 1952; Coleman 1966; Herriott and St.

John 1966). Corwin and Schmit (1970) found that twice as many inner-city teachers (compared with teachers outside the inner city) requested placement transfers and that 45 percent of these requests came from first and second year teachers.

Several studies have indicated that teachers tend to establish a set of expectations about the child's academic capabilities and behavior, based on social criteria and hearsay evidence, without firsthand interaction with the child (Rist 1970; Rosenthal and Jacobson 1968).

One possible question arising from these studies concerns the type of teacher training offered at the university level. While it is unfair to focus on the poor quality of teacher training as the sole cause of problems which exist in the urban classroom, it is evident that a lack of understanding of the community, poor communication with the parents, inflexibility in altering teaching practices to suit the needs of the inner-city child, and inappropriate values and attitudes, all combine to impede the educational experiences of the inner-city child.

Traditional programs for educating teachers have included a smattering of courses centered on urban education (urban sociology, the "disadvantaged child," and the inner-city child). Programs of this nature tend to concentrate on the use of numerous theoretical texts concerned with educating the inner-city child. One theory is often advocated over another (Bereiter and Englemann 1966; Morine and Morine 1970; Smith and Geoffrey 1968). Student teachers tend to express confusion concerning the appropriateness and educational values of the methods presented in these texts.

Courses have been varied by the introduction of popular books which provide a personal account of the author's trials and tribulations within the inner-city school (Daniels 1973; Dennison 1969; Herndon 1968; Koch 1970; Kozol 1967). Teacher trainees tend to relate to these books more readily but often fail to develop their own personal philosophy for inner-city teaching.

Several universities have initiated model classrooms for inner-city children within the university setting (e.g., Institute for Developmental Studies), while others have developed preemployment training programs directed at the new graduate (e.g., Western Michigan University). Miller and Woock (1973) report that attitudes toward low socioeconomic status children and parents substantially improved after a fifteen-week training session. It has been the authors' experience that programs which fail to integrate inner-city field placements and observational assignments into the course of study fail to significantly change teacher attitudes toward these children. One of the primary purposes of the authors' recent study was to empirically test this hypothesis.

In 1974, research was begun in Montreal to explore the manner in which inner-city and suburban children perceived and used the resources in their own environment (Jacobs 1975). The results indicated that inner-city and suburban children expressed their values, attitudes, interests, and needs in a similar manner. Interviews revealed that suburban teachers tend to perceive a much more pleasant environment than the suburban child described, while inner-city teachers offered impressions of gloom, despair, and depression which were seldom expressed by inner-city children.

Thus, the object of the authors' recent study was to provide an in-depth view of both the teacher's and the child's perspective of the inner-city environment. Several questions were posed:

1. Would the teacher's perception of the inner-city child's environment match the child's own perception?

2. If a mismatch existed, would the teacher be able to alter his or her perceptions by discarding the myths in which he or she believed?

3. Could the use of a questionnaire, mapping and videotaping paths followed to school, and photographing the child's home range (area where the child lives, plays, and goes to school) be a satisfactory method of recording the child's perception of his or her environment?

4. Would the use of the above-mentioned materials help to alter the teacher's perceptions of the child's environment where a mismatch of perceptions existed?

METHOD

Subjects

The subjects were 78 children from elementary and secondary inner-city schools in Montreal. The children ranged in age from four years to nineteen years with a mean age of ten years four months. The group consisted of 34 males and 44 females.

The inner-city population in Montreal can be divided into two distinct groups: (1) first generation immigrants (e.g., Greek, Chinese, Portuguese, Italian, West Indian) from a low socioeconomic level; and (2) second and third generation Canadians from a low socioeconomic level. In this study, 73 percent of the children were first generation immigrants and 27 percent were second and third generation Canadians.

The teachers chosen for this study were enrolled in courses in the education department of Concordia University. These university students were classified within three distinct units: (1) those with no exposure (no university training in inner-city education, N = 15); (2) those with limited exposure (one university course on inner-city education with a limited fieldwork component, N = 13); (3) those with extensive exposure (a specific course on the inner-city child with field research and a placement component, N = 9).

Instruments

A detailed questionnaire was developed to examine the child's perceptions of his or her environment. The items in the questionnaire sought to determine in depth the child's perceptions of home, neighborhood, family, peer group, school, and, in general, the child's life-style. Detailed biographical data were obtained from this questionnaire.

Included in the questionnaire were seven questions designed to elicit from the children a nonverbal response about their feelings con-cerning their environment. The children were required to respond to each question by circling the picture of the face which most closely repre-sented their feelings (Fig. 1). Administration time for this interview was approximately one hour.

Figure 1. Faces Presented for Nonverbal Expression of Feelings

Procedure

Students enrolled in a university course (Ur-ban Child) were instructed to explore specific aspects of the inner-city community in accor-dance with a course outline. These students were then instructed to administer the ques-tionnaire to ten children in their respective schools. The questionnaire was administered to each child individually and his or her answers were responded to with a nod of acceptance. The questionnaire was then administered to the three groups of students who were required to respond to the questions as they thought an inner-city child might. This concluded the for-mal collection of data.

RESULTS

An analysis of the data clearly indicates that students with minimal exposure to the inner-city environment and those having few personal interactions with inner-city children tend to view life in the inner-city in terms of extreme poverty, deprivation, degradation, despair, gloom, and depression. A detailed analysis of the responses of students having no university training in inner-city education revealed a marked misperception of the environment com-pared with the perceptions of inner-city chil-dren. The students' preconceived notions of the child's home environment (e.g., where the child sleeps, his or her family life, eating patterns, possessions) as being one of degradation and poverty corroborates the stereotyped view of inner-city life. They fail to see the many positive experiences that these children have had (e.g., use of public transportation—buses, trains, boats—and travel—visits to museums, commu-nity camps, and summer park programs). In ad-dition, they tend to view the neighborhood as one that is filled with factories, busy and un-clean streets, and where the children are com-pelled to play in the streets and alleys. In con-trast, those students with university training, which included a course on the urban child, field placements, and observational assign-ments, tend to have perceptions which more closely approximate the child's perception of his or her environment.

TABLE 1. Percentages of Responses to Item 1—Where Child Lives

Responses	😊	😐	🙁	😠	No Reply
No Training	0	67	20	13	0
Training	7	70	23	0	0
Training and Placement and In-depth Analysis	56	44	0	0	0
Inner-City Children	59	17	12	0	12

Table 1 indicates the responses by inner-city children and the university students to the questions which required the subjects to circle the face which most accurately represented their feelings about living in the inner city. Clearly, the perceptions of those students having optimal exposure most closely approximate the perceptions of the inner-city children. However, the accuracy of their perceptions for the way in which children feel about their street is less clear (Table 2). Reactions to school and teachers can be seen in Table 3 and Table 4. Here again, those who had university training, placement, and observational assignments appear to have the most accurate perceptions. However, in both cases, these students tend to overestimate the children's perception by assigning a more positive rating than the children did.

The analysis of the data clearly indicates that the child's perception of his or her environment is most closely matched by the student having optimal training. Those university students with a minimal field placement appear to perceive the inner-city environment from a perspective of gloom and despair. However, their perceptions are far less negative than those students having had neither training nor experience in inner-city education.

TABLE 2. Percentages of Responses to Item 2—The Child's Street

Responses	😊	😐	🙁	😠	No Reply
No Training	27	40	13	13	7
Training	8	62	15	15	0
Training and Placement and In-depth Analysis	22	52	22	0	4
Inner-City Children	41	30	10	6	13

TABLE 3. Percentages of Responses to Item 5—The Child's School

Responses	😊	😐	🙁	😠	No Reply
No Training	20	40	20	20	0
Training	15	39	23	23	0
Training and Placement and In-depth Analysis	78	22	0	0	0
Inner-City Children	53	23	8	3	13

TABLE 4. Percentages of Responses to Item 6—The Child's Teacher

Responses	😊	😐	🙁	😠	No Reply
No Training	0	20	13	60	7
Training	30	39	8	23	0
Training and Placement and In-depth Analysis	78	22	0	0	0
Inner-City Children	62	12	6	8	12

DISCUSSION

The results of the authors' recent study support the contention that teacher perceptions will more closely approximate the inner-city child's perceptions when fieldwork placements and observational assignments are integral components of the teacher training program. In addition, the results clearly indicate that the teacher interviews with the inner-city children (an essential part of the observational assignment) have been instrumental in providing more accurate information about the inner city than short field assignments.

Rist (1970) has noted that teachers tend to receive, on an informal basis, social information about their students. Reports from social workers and other teachers who have had previous experience with the child and/or siblings tend to influence the teacher's perceptions and expectations of the child. Data and information concerning each child should be individually collected, allowing for a more accurate perception of the child's world.

The environment in each inner-city area in Montreal differs considerably. As a result, the perceptions of the residents differ, thereby necessitating flexibility of instructional methods and curriculum. The relevancy of curricula must take into account familiar environmental factors as well as the expressed needs and interests of the child.

Miller and Woock (1973) have suggested that training teachers in behavioral techniques may be more effective and beneficial than attempting to change their attitudes and misperceptions. However, in order to effectively provide meaningful reinforcement for the child, one necessary prerequisite might be a more realistic understanding of the child's environment.

The use of field placements and observational assignments in conjunction with a program which requires several in-depth interviews with inner-city children appears to be a successful adjunct to traditional courses in inner-city education. In fact, the interviewing technique which allows the teacher to delve into the child's personal world has provided an ideal method for demythologizing many false assumptions. If teacher perceptions are altered to more closely approximate those of the child (as the data would tend to indicate), future research should be directed toward the evaluation of changes in teaching methodologies and/or curriculum innovations. If relevancy of curriculum is a necessary correlate for academic and affective growth within the inner city, then demythologizing the erroneous myths and stereotypes that exist can only yield more positive results.

References

Becker, H. "The Career of the Chicago Public School Teacher." *American Journal of Sociology* 57 (1952): 470-477.

Bereiter, C., and Englemann, S. *Teaching Disadvantaged Children in the Preschool.* Englewood Cliffs, N.J.: Prentice-Hall, 1966.

Coleman, J. S., et al. *Equal Educational Opportunity.* Washington, D.C.: U.S. Office of Education, Government Printing Office, 1966.

Corwin, R. G., and Schmit, M. "Teachers in Inner City Schools." *Education and Urban Society* 2 (1970): 131-155.

Daniels, S. *How 2 Gerbils, 20 Goldfish, 200 Games, 2,000 Books and I Taught Them How To Read.* Philadelphia: Westminster Press, 1973.

Dennison, G. *The Lives of Children.* New York: Random House, 1969.

Ginsburg, H. *The Myth of the Deprived Child.* Englewood Cliffs, N.J.: Prentice-Hall, 1972.

Herndon, J. *The Way It Spozed To Be.* New York: Simon and Schuster, 1968.

Herriott, R., and St. John, N. H. *Social Class and the Urban School.* New York: John Wiley & Sons, 1966.

Jacobs, E. *Developing Teacher Awareness of the Young Child's Urban Environment.* Presented at United States Department of Agriculture Forest Services Conference—"Children, Nature and the Urban Environment"—May 1975, Washington, D.C.

Koch, K. *Wishes, Lies and Dreams.* New York: Chelsea House Publishers, 1970.

Kohl, H. *36 Children.* New York: New American Library, 1967.

Kozol, J. *Death at an Early Age.* Boston: Houghton Mifflin, 1967.

Miller, H. L., and Woock, R. R. *Social Foundations of Urban Education.* New York: Holt, Rinehart and Winston, 1973.

Morine, H., and Morine, G. *A Primer for the Inner City School.* New York: McGraw-Hill, 1970.

Rist, R. C. "Student Social Class and Teacher Expectations: The Self-Fulfilling Prophecy in Ghetto Education." *Harvard Educational Review* 10 (August 1970): 411-451.

Rosenthal, R., and Jacobson, L. *Pygmalion in the Classroom.* New York: Holt, Rinehart and Winston, 1968.

Smith, L. M., and Geoffrey, W. *The Complexities of an Urban Classroom.* New York: Holt, Rinehart and Winston, 1968.

Charles E. Billiard, Joan M. Elifson,
and John W. Rubadeau

Attitudes about Nonstandard Dialects Can Be Changed

Until the mid-1960s sociolinguists had not provided a linguistic analysis of a Black dialect in America for educators' use. When these early analyses were made available, one would have hoped that pedagogical methodology for dealing with language learning problems associated with Black dialect would have followed immediately. However, English instruction in this area has not changed in spite of research findings (Lin 1965). There are at least three reasons for this gap between knowledge and implementation that require comment. First, an attitudinal problem exists; second, a philosophical dilemma stands in the way of clear-cut decisions about dialectally different students; and third, research has not produced conclusive answers about "what works."

ATTITUDINAL PROBLEM

Black speech, a social dialect, has become stigmatized. Long associated with groups at the bottom of the socioeconomic ladder, it has come to be labeled "sloppy, illiterate" speech (Plaister 1967; Bereiter 1966). In spite of the fact that linguists label it "different," a majority of middle class Americans still see it as "deficient" (Stewart 1967; Ney 1971).

Even such a well-known Black linguist as Charles G. Hurst, Jr., has described the Black English speech of Negro freshmen at Howard University as being

. . . defective speech . . . abnormal speech . . . [which consists of] oral aberrations . . . phonetic distortions, defective syntax, misarticulations, mispronunciations, limited or poor vocabulary, and faulty phonology. (1965, pp. 1-2)

Labov elaborates on what the critics of nonstandard speech mean by "deficiency":

The viewpoint which has been widely accepted and used as the basis for large-scale intervention programs is that the children show a cultural deficit as a result of an impoverished environment in their early years. A great deal of attention has been given to language. In this area the deficit theory appears as the notion of verbal deprivation: black children from the ghetto area are said to receive little verbal stimulation, to hear very little well-formed language and as a result are impoverished in their means of verbal expression. It is said that they cannot speak complete sentences, do not know the names of common objects, cannot form concepts or convey logical thoughts. (1972, p. 59)

Baratz suggests why many psychologists concluded that Black children speak a "non-language," and calls attention to the basic error.

[The] basic problem was that [the] measures of "language development" were measures based on standard English. . . . From these [it was] concluded that since black children do not speak standard English, they must be deficient in language development. The linguists for their part have described the differences between Negro non-standard and standard English in some detail. . . . All the linguists studying Negro non-standard agree that these differences are systematized structured rules with the vernacular. . . . This [is] language difference not deficiency, (1969), p. 99)

And Labov summarizes the stance of the linguists who hold that Black nonstandard English is merely different and lacks nothing as a language system (except perhaps social status).

Linguists are in an excellent position to demonstrate the fallacies of the verbal deprivation theory. All linguists agree that nonstandard dialects are highly structured systems; they do not see these dialects as accumulations of errors caused by the failure of their speakers to master standard English. When linguists hear black children saying "he crazy" or "her my friend" they do not hear a primitive language. Nor do they believe that the speech of working class people is merely a form of emotional expression incapable of relating logical thought. Linguists therefore condemn with a single voice Bereiter's view that the vernacular can be disregarded. (1972, p. 67)

Though for the academicians the debate has subsided, with the linguists making the stronger case, many practitioners in the public schools have not altered behavior in accordance with the equalitarian view of language divergence (Lin 1965, p. 5).

PHILOSOPHICAL DILEMMA

The second factor slowing the implementation of linguists' findings is a philosophical dilemma. Those who have accepted the validity of the Black dialect for a particular social context debate the school's responsibility to Black English speakers. Some argue that the school should eradicate the dialect, in spite of its linguistic equality with other dialects of English including the standard (Zale 1972; Rafferty 1967). They argue that because of its social stigma, it can only handicap the student.

At the other extreme are those who argue that the Black dialect speakers should be taught in their own dialect with no effort made to change their speech. They charge that any other stand is biased, even prejudiced, in favor of standard White speech (Sledd 1969; O'Neil 1968). Moreover, they argue it should be paramount that educators teach the general population an equalitarian attitude toward language.

Finally, between these extreme views are those educators who believe that Black students cannot eliminate their home speech, even if that would be desired, but that they can add to their verbal repertoire a second variety of English— the standard dialect. Such an accomplishment would produce bidialectal speakers (Lin 1965; Mantell 1973; Allen 1973; Shuy 1972).

There is strong support for each philosophical stand. Although it is difficult to identify a trend in favor of one or the other stand, the arguments of the bidialectalists appear to dominate the literature and seem to be the most cogent. Bidialectalists argue that no attempt to alter the language of the nonstandard dialect speakers is just as prejudiced as to attempt to alter it radically. Not to challenge the users of nonstandard speech to learn a second dialect limits their access to the mainstream of American life and tends to solidify segregation. Yet, to ask children to "forget" the language of home and neighborhood is to ask them to divorce themselves from their way of life. Lin further suggests:

The dialect, no matter how other people may judge it, has evidently proved socially and psychologically satisfactory to the individual who uses it. . . . It is . . . a symbol of security and love. It is the language of his initiation into life. . . . Take that away from him and he will be . . . an individual with no identity. (1965, p. 2)

While offering access to the world beyond the home, bidialectalism need not disparage the child's home language.

LIMITATIONS OF RESEARCH

Educators have been handicapped in implementing the most recent linguistic findings concerning dialects, because research findings have not shown a clear-cut method or curriculum for achieving the desired results in either the case of bidialectalism or "eradication" of nonstandard speech. A number of projects have been conducted, however, that have sought to test ways of developing the ability to switch dialect codes among students who speak a nonstandard dialect (Golden 1962; Lin 1965; Mantell 1973), but none have produced conclusive findings.

Attitudes

It is our feeling that the attitudes that teachers, particularly English instructors, hold toward nonstandard dialect is crucial. From a practitioner's point of view, solving that problem must precede a decision about philosophical issues or the implementation of pedagogical techniques, if some surefire ones become known. We have sought, within the context of teacher training, to broaden the knowledge base of teachers about Black nonstandard dialect and foster more positive attitudes about that dialect so that teachers are more likely to accept the Black student's speech for what it is—a legitimate, systematic, rule-governed dialect of English.

RESEARCH

Actually, we are presenting here four research investigations which were carried out to see if attitude change could be generated in a class within one quarter's time. Charles Billiard conducted two investigations: one using graduate students who were enrolled in a social dialects class at Georgia State University and who were engaged in dialect fieldwork; and another with Robert Driscoll, which ran in three consecutive quarters during the 1974-75 school year with preservice teachers who were student teaching in the Atlanta Public School System. John Rubadeau was interested in investigating a change in attitudes that might result from cognitive input; therefore, using transformation grammar as a tool, he examined with his students the ways in which both standard and Black dialects are systematic and rule-governed. Joan Elifson replicated Rubadeau's experimental treatment but used graduate students, all with teaching experience, as subjects. All of the students were enrolled in a course in social dialects.

Billiard's Dialect Fieldwork Study

As we have pointed out, a considerable lag exists between linguistic knowledge of dialect varieties in American English and actual classroom practices dealing with language learning problems of students speaking nonstandard English, particularly those speaking nonstandard Black dialects. The following study describes an attempt to use fieldwork in dialectology as a method to expand the teacher's knowledge of Black dialect vocabulary, to enhance his or her respect for Black dialects, and to increase awareness of language variation across various dimensions.

For teachers and students working together, the study of regional and social dialects offers unlimited opportunities to open the four walls of the classroom to the outside world. Through fieldwork in dialectology, students can discover ways in which language both promotes and destroys human understanding. Exploration of dialects, followed by careful analysis of data, will often reveal principles of language useful to the teacher in battling language prejudices in the classroom and community. An even greater importance of the fieldworker's encounter with the informant is the strong probability of the interviewer's discovery of another individual's humanity.

Furthermore, few disciplines, to the extent offered by dialectology, encourage students and teachers to immerse themselves in basic and applied research, theoretical speculation and practical application, and a synthesis of subject matter ranging across such fields as geography, history, sociology, psychology, linguistics, and literature.

To exploit these teaching-learning potentialities, a course at Georgia State University entitled "Social Dialects and Language Learning" is attempting to make contributions to the Linguistic Atlas of the Gulf States (LAGS) Project and, at the same time, is working toward practical applications of dialectology in teacher education. This graduate elective course, taken primarily by English, reading, and elementary teachers, proposes the following objectives that can be expressed as statements about language attitudes, skills, and knowledge.

1. Inferences concerning the social, ethnic, and cultural significance of dialect differences should be based on careful observation of actual usage.

2. Sensitivity to variations of speech reflecting geography, racial identity, socioeconomic status (SES), sex, age, and occupation should free the teacher from the right-wrong dichotomy and enable the teacher and students to make judgments of language usage on the basis of appropriateness for the occasion.

3. The knowledge that usage is not fixed but changes and that it is not completely uniform, even at the most highly educated levels, should make untenable any claim to moral sanction for a particular usage.

4. An application of knowledge of dialect variations should enable the teacher to deal more effectively with reading, writing, speaking, and listening problems of students.

5. Recognizing that a person's language is an intimate possession, the teacher will encourage oral and written expression without censorship and will attempt to cultivate respect and admiration for the dialects of minority groups in the community.

The opportunity to realize some of the foregoing objectives resulted from an invitation to the instructor and students to assist in developing urban vocabulary work sheets to supplement the LAGS work sheets. These work sheets, experimental and inventorial in nature, are now undergoing a second revision with a third round of use and refinement planned in the near future. The content of these work sheets, far from being intuitive in origin, derives largely from other Linguistic Atlas projects, particularly from the cultural outline of 32 categories established by Kurath (1939) for the *Handbook of the Linguistic Geography of New England* and the adaptations made from Kurath's work by Pederson for the Chicago work sheets used in his study "The Pronunciation of English in Metropolitan Chicago."

Although the use of Linguistic Atlas work sheets as a frame of reference for urban vocabulary surveys has been criticized as not reflecting urban culture, theoretical considerations and actual data justify the use of the Linguistic Atlas framework. First, the student fieldworkers in Atlanta are eliciting useful responses to most of the more than two hundred items on the work sheets; second, the survey gives a sampling of the Atlanta speech community back to the late 1880s.

Classroom procedures and activities were organized into five cumulative, related phases to prepare the students for conducting useful fieldwork for the revision of the urban work sheets and for concurrently achieving major objectives of the course. These approaches are flexible and could be modified for use at various educational levels.

In the first phase of the work, students were asked to write a linguistic autobiography. How do speech patterns come to be what they are? Such factors as their birthplace, education, travel, and occupation of parents, grandparents, husband or wife, and close friends were examined. Also, the students considered their intellectual interests, travel, and work experiences as they speculated about regional and social aspects of their speech. One student remarked, "I now feel a greater pride in my language heritage. I used to be ashamed of my speech." Another said, "I would like to be able to adapt to different social situations more readily."

Small groups in the class were formed for the second phase of the work, which was aimed at expanding the students' awareness of phonological, lexical, and grammatical contrasts in the idiolects. One activity involved having members read set passages which included such contrasting regional features as the presence or loss of postvocalic /r/; difference or similarity among the stressed vowels of *Mary, merry,* and *marry;* the contrastive use of /z/ or /s/ in *Mrs.* In addition, groups of two interviewed each other using sections from the LAGS work sheets closely related in content to the experimental urban work sheets. This practice interviewing enabled students to anticipate some of the problems in actual interviewing situations and to read purposefully "Field Procedures: Instructions for Investigators, Linguistic Atlas of the Gulf States" (McDavid 1974). The range and depth of questioning about language variations seemed to be growing as evidenced in this tenth grade English teacher's troubled introspection: "I can accept many dialects intellectually, but emotionally I still believe there is a more or less correct way to speak."

Next came the preparation for the actual fieldwork. Instructional priorities and adequate sampling procedures had to be reconciled. In order to insure that each student had the experience of interviewing a person of another ethnic group, each member of the class was asked to complete two interviews: one with a White informant, another with a Black informant. In a few instances, data collecting was incomplete and probably even inaccurate. However, the experience was worth the possible loss of data. In one instance, a ninety-three-year-old Black woman stopped the White interviewer halfway through the questionnaire, saying, "I don't want to answer no more questions, but I'd like you to come visit me again."

Beyond planning for an equal number of Black and White informants, the class used the Linguistic Atlas types of informants with minor modifications: Type I—little formal education, 60 years of age or older; Type II—high school education, 40 to 59 years of age; Type III—college education, 20 to 39 years of age; Type IV—generally high school education or less, under 20 years of age. Approximately the same number of females and males were interviewed. Also, a socioeconomic-geographic sampling of the Atlanta metropolitan area was attempted to include the following kinds of communities: middle to upper-middle SES Black; middle to upper-middle SES White; inner city, integrated low to middle SES Black and White; and low to middle SES rural neighborhoods.

Although not all interviews were pleasant experiences, the consensus of reactions to the fieldwork seems to be captured by the student who said, "I had the feeling of having visited a person I had known for many years." For teachers who usually talk too much in the classroom, the experience of listening more than talking may have been an enlightening and wholesome discovery of how much other people know, especially those who are unsophisticated. Also, since each class member had interviewed two informants of different ethnic groups, each person had become more sensitive to vocabulary variations between Black and White informants.

Two classes had conducted a total of 101 interviews using questionnaires listing 214 items. Each informant had given an average of approximately four responses to each item, counting both active and passive responses. A passive response was a synonym the informant had heard but did not use. The data consisted of about 86,000 lexical items.

Since the questionnaires were coded by SES, racial identity, age, and sex, the students agreed that they could sort the questionnaires into these categories. Each set of questionnaires was scanned to identify certain lexical items that seemed to elicit different responses rather consistently, then the number of responses for each of these items was counted.

To determine whether the data supported vocabulary variation by SES, the students selected the semantic category of "important neighborhoods." In Table 1, Buttermilk Bottom is the name of a Black ghetto that has been almost completely replaced by an urban renewal project known as Bedford Pines. West Paces Ferry is a White upper SES neighborhood; "Roccocola" denotes a part of the same community. A White ghetto of Atlanta is known as Cabbage Town and sometimes more generally as the Grant Park Area. A count of active and passive responses (passive responses are indicated in parentheses) shows that a familiarity with place names is strongly associated with SES. One strange inconsistency is the relatively large number of low-middle SES and upper-middle SES informants who have heard the term *Buttermilk Bottom*. One interviewer accidently stumbled across a probable explanation: the recent popularity of a folk song entitled "Buttermilk Bottom."

Table 1. Vocabulary Variation by Socioeconomic Status: Lower, Lower-Middle, Upper-Middle SES.

Lexical Items	LSES	LMSES	UMSES
Buttermilk Bottom	6 (8)	2 (4)	0 (5)
Bedford Pines	10 (5)	9 (5)	15(14)
West Paces Ferry	2(16)	15(10)	25 (0)
"Roccocola"	0 (0)	0 (2)	3 (7)
Cabbage Town	9 (4)	5(12)	2 (3)
Grant Park Area	5 (3)	12 (9)	21 (4)

The semantic categories of social parties, hair styles, and food are among many that show vocabulary variation by racial identity. Beyond organizing and managing data, students should be encouraged to speculate and hypothesize about the data. Why does *hoedown* show up so strongly in both the Black and White passive vocabulary? Several students suggested the data reflect the impact of the popular television show "Hee Haw." In addition to *shine bones*, meats common in the diets of many Black families are *pig feet, pig tails, pig ears;* whereas *pork chops* and *bacon*, more expensive cuts of meat, are common in the diet of many White families. Table 2 summarizes some the semantic categories that vary by racial identity.

Table 2. Vocabulary Variation by Racial Caste

Lexical Items	Black Informants	White Informants
Social party		
party	24(20)	44 (0)
gig	43 (7)	6(24)
hoedown	3(32)	20(25)
Hair styles		
fro	49 (0)	11(31)
bun	8(20)	20(22)
Food		
pork chops	20(16)	41 (0)
shine bones	26(17)	5(12)

Semantic categories selected for the purpose of examining vocabulary variation by age are houses and the Black financial districts in Atlanta. The *shotgun house* and *railroad house* both designate a house of three rooms arranged in a row so that one could look through the front door and see out the back door or fire a shotgun through the front door and scatter pellets out the back door. The *dog trot house*, improperly described by all but one informant, labels a house made up of two separate rooms joined together by a roof. The open space covered by a roof between the two rooms was used as a shelter for animals.

The single passive response to the name *Wheat Street* reflects the fact that *Wheat Street* was renamed Auburn Avenue in 1893. Auburn Avenue reached its zenith as the Black financial center of Atlanta in the 1920s. During this time it was called "Sweet Auburn." In recent years,

Table 3. Vocabulary Variation by Age

Lexical Items	>60 yrs.	40-59 yrs.	20-39 yrs.	<20 yrs.
Houses				
shot gun house	5(14)	2(5)	0 (4)	0(0)
railroad house	3(10)	3(4)	0 (2)	0(0)
dog trot house	2 (5)	1(3)	0 (0)	0(0)
Black financial districts				
Wheat Street	0 (1)	0(0)	0 (0)	0(0)
Auburn Avenue	16 (5)	10(8)	7(10)	5(6)
"Sweet Auburn"	7(10)	2(7)	1 (6)	0(8)
Cascade Area	7(12)	15(9)	18 (4)	20(5)

Auburn Avenue has deteriorated and new Black financial centers have arisen in the Cascade Area and other areas as reflected by the vocabulary variation by age in Table 3.

One of the more surprising outcomes of the survey to members of the class was the extent of vocabulary variation by sex. The semantic categories selected to investigate language variation between the sexes were *food*, *pimp*, and *prostitute*. Students speculated that the greater discrimination by females would be in naming foods.

Speculation among the students concerning the variations in usage between men and women in the use of the terms *lady of the night* and *whore* centered around the question of unequal status of men and women in American society. The preference of women for *lady of the night* was viewed as a euphemistic disclaimer of a role they should not and would not have to play in a society if women had equality with men. Furthermore, it was argued that men in choosing the vilifying term *whore* were expressing contempt for women and an attitude that human beings are for the use of other more powerful individuals.

To summarize this approach to dialectology as a process of discovery, the procedure and activities have involved the following sequence: (1) the discovery by individual students of some sources of their linguistic behavior, (2) the discovery of dialect contrasts in the speech of members of a small group, (3) the use of a questionnaire as an instrument for investigating the language usage of others, (4) the organization and management of language data for investigating the variation of language in several dimensions, and (5) speculation about the causes of language variation in terms of historical, geographic, social, and psychological factors.

If children learn through the wise practice and attitudes of their teachers to respect the speech of others, we may have one of the most promising ways of combating language prejudice in our next adult generation.

The preceding method of instruction was subjected to statistical analysis. Two similar groups, a control group and an experimental group given the foregoing treatment, were posttested using the Black Intelligence Test of Cultural Homogeneity. The results of the analysis are shown in Table 4.

Table 4. t-Test for Experimental and Control Groups

Experimental Group   *Control Group*

Whites: N = 21, X̄ = 65.05, SD = 7.12, t* = 4.69, df = 39; Control: N = 20, X̄ = 55.3, SD = 6.16

*critical t value for α = .05 is 2.021

Blacks: N = 6, X̄ = 84.33, SD = 5.05, t* = .269, df = 9; Control: N = 5, X̄ = 82.64, SD = 14.89

*critical t value for α = .05 is 2.262

Whites in 20% + Integrated Schools for Two Yrs.+ : N = 8, X̄ = 66.62, SD = 4.53

In Table 4, the statistics show that the White teachers in the experimental group who were exposed to the treatment differed significantly (α= .05) from those in the control group, as was hypothesized. It was also hypothesized that Black teachers would have higher mean scores as a group than White teachers, and Black teachers would differ little between experimental and control groups. This hypothesis was supported, as can be seen in Table 4, with a t-test that is not significant at the $\alpha = .05$ level.

Furthermore, the group of White teachers who were not given any treatment but had been teaching in integrated schools with a 20 percent or higher Black enrollment for two or more years did as well on the instrument as those Whites in the experimental group who were exposed to the treatment.

Driscoll and Billiard's Study with Student Teachers

In an experiment using taped interviews of elementary school children in Atlanta Public Schools, Driscoll and Billiard attempted to change attitudes and affect practices of preservice elementary teachers. During a three-school-quarter experiment, 15 to 18 student teachers assigned each quarter to an inner-city teaching center in Atlanta were randomly placed in experimental and control groups. The control groups were given no formal instruction in dialects; rather, they were given an intensive ten-day training in lesson and unit planning, mini-lesson presentations followed by post-analysis, classroom observations, and community studies. On the other hand, the experimental groups were involved in a study of the nature of dialect variation and specific investigation of dialect features of Atlanta elementary school children. From listening to a random sampling of tapes of informal and formal speech of middle SES Black and White and low SES Black and White Atlanta students in grades one through six, the experimental group identified the following features as occuring more frequently in the speech of the low SES Blacks than in the speech of the other groups.

1. Possession by juxtaposition (instead of genitive *'s*)
   "in his brother room"

2. Invariant *be*
   before adjectives: "I be scared."
   before adverbs: "I be out dere. . . ."
   as progressive present: "I still be swimmin'."

3. Zero copula
   with adjectives: "Boy, John, you crazy!"
   with adverbs: "Now she over at the funeral home."

4. Past tense unmarked
   "I ask 'em if a policeman come in and he go past the cop and he say. . . ."

5. *Them* as a demonstrative
   "Them girl was mad."

6. *What* as a relative pronoun
   "I like to go up on that thing what goes around in the air."

7. Existential *it*
   "It was a snake in there hangin' on top."

8. Multiple negation
   ". . . if nobody don't play with me."

9. Pleonastic or appositive pronoun
   "My daddy's brother he was sittin'. . . ."

10. Absence of the plural suffix
    "She took ten pencil."

11. Progressive verb + *in*
    ". . . the first thing I know he bitin' his hand."

12. *Gonna* used as purposeful future
    "You gonna get a whippin'."

13. Third person singular present tense
    "She dive into the water."

Based on these listening experiences, the experimental group members became increasingly aware of the systematic occurrence of specific dialect features of the low SES Black speakers. Furthermore, the student teachers noted the vivid, colorful quality and rhetorical effectiveness of the low SES Black children's speech. For example, in telling ghost stories these children not only used concrete nouns and vivid verbs but also structured their stories with a provocative beginning, rising action, and exciting climax.

Both control and experimental groups were pretested and posttested to determine change, if any, in attitude toward dialect variations of pronunciation and grammar. A dialect test tape composed of phonological and grammatical variants observed in the speech of Atlanta elementary school students was played for both experimental and control groups. The student teachers were asked to record their reactions to these speech variants on a semantic differential scale labeled with the opposite terms *educated, uneducated*. Segments on the scale were marked as "strongly agree," "agree," "neutral," "disagree," and "strongly disagree." Thus students recorded their subjective evaluation of potentially critical dialect features by recording their response on the semantic differential scale. Each section of the scale was assigned a numerical value so that scores for each student and mean scores for control and experimental groups could be determined.

Using the mean scores on the language attitude test *(educated/uneducated scale)*, a significant difference at $\alpha = .05$ favoring the experimental group was found with the t-test for the overall analysis. These results could be interpreted to mean that the experimental group had become more unbiased in accepting divided usage forms common among educated speakers.

To determine whether a change in attitude toward nonstandard Black English resulted in changed teacher behavior in the classroom, the students in both groups were asked to tape record lessons taught at regular intervals throughout the quarter. These tapes are being analyzed in terms of teacher responses to student language production by using the following categories: (1) positive reinforcement by the student teacher of a student's reading in nonstandard dialect, (2) positive reinforcement by the student teacher of a student's oral expression in free class discussion, (3) negative criticism of a student's reading in nonstandard dialect, (4) negative criticism of a student's oral

expression in free class discussion. Preliminary analysis of these data indicates a trend of more positive teacher behavior toward nonstandard dialect in the classroom situation.

Rubadeau's Study

Rationale: Rubadeau built his study on the premise that a change in the knowledge of teachers would effect a change in attitudes. He believed that a demonstration of the systematic nature of Black dialect would cause a change in the value system of preservice teachers.

He maintained that by illustrating the similarity between the two forms of speech, he could prove to the prospective teacher that Black English shares the fundamental patterns and logic of standard English. Its variant form derives not from "sloppiness" in its structure or from a genetic bent on the part of the speaker toward "illiteracy," but rather from regular, consistent grammatical rules.

He designed a series of ten one-hour lessons showing the similarities between standard and nonstandard dialect. He used transformational grammar as the tool for showing the similarities. The deep structures (basic meaning level of language) of several sentences were shown, using an overhead projector, and their transformations to surface structure (the level of speech or writing) were traced. The rules of both dialects that govern the transformations were shown to be similar in nature and use.

It was hoped that these lessons would create enough cognitive dissonance so that the teacher would have to make some cognitive adjustment in order to collate this new linguistic information into his or her present attitudes and beliefs. One of Festinger's (1966) major hypotheses is that "the existence of dissonance being psychologically uncomfortable will motivate the person to try to reduce the dissonance and achieve consonance" (p. 3). In order, therefore, to achieve consonance (consistency), the prospective teacher would change his or her attitudes toward Black English based upon new information. Once this change was made, dissonance would be reduced and intellectual perception of Black English and the teacher's attitude toward Black English would tend to be more harmonious.

Indeed, this is not an unrealistic expectation; Festinger writes that "our behavior and feelings are frequently modified in accordance with new information" (1966, p. 19). Thus, if the prospective teacher can be shown that the similarities of deep structures and their transformations appropriate to Black and standard English generate distinctly different surface structures, then he or she should be more inclined to have favorable attitudes toward Black English. At the very least, the teacher will have to make some attitudinal adjustments in order to deal with this new information.

The Experimental Design: The population from which the sample groups were drawn was composed of Georgia State University elementary education majors. Two sections of the course "Language Arts in the Elementary School" were taught winter quarter 1975. Rubadeau arbitrarily chose one section as his experimental group and one as the control group.

In order not to bias the results, both instructors of the courses did not teach anything related to attitudes toward language or Black dialect until the treatment condition was completed and the posttest had been given.

The research design followed a modified Solomon-Four design (Campbell and Stanley 1970). Although complete randomization is called for in this design, the situation at Georgia State University during this time did not lend itself to a completely "pure" implementation of the Solomon-Four Group Design as the classes came intact. The classes were arbitrarily assigned to the experimental and control groups, and randomly assigned to be pretested or not.

Hypothesis: Rubadeau tested the following hypothesis:

A. *Experimental hypothesis*

Those students who are taught transformational grammar rules illustrating that the deep structure of Black English and standard English is the same will have significantly more positive attitudes toward Black English than the control group as measured by an attitudinal survey.

B. *Null hypothesis*

Those students who are taught transformational grammar rules illustrating that the deep structure of Black English and standard English is the same will not change their attitudes toward Black English.

The Measures: The test of language attitudes is divided into two parts: Part I was conceived to be a basic measure of peoples' attitudes toward language. Part II was conceived to be a basic measure of peoples' knowledge about Black dialect.

The core of Part I (questions 1 through 72) was taken from the *Language Inquiry Test* developed by Frogner (1969) under a United States Office of Education grant. This test was devised to measure teachers' attitudes toward standard English and English usage. Frogner enlisted the aid of ten well-known linguists, among whom were Ravin I. McDavid, Harold B. Allen, Jean Malmstrom, and Albert Marckwardt, in constructing and validating her instrument.

Eleven questions from an attitude test, administered at a preconvention workshop of the 1974 national convention of the National Council of Teachers of English by Lou Kelly, Iowa State University, were randomly incorporated into Frogner's inventory.

Because Rubadeau was only interested in teachers' attitudes toward Black English, many of the items on Frogner's and Kelly's tests were irrelevant. Hence, a committee of five people conversant with the field of Black English and sociolinguistics eliminated irrelevant items. With unanimous agreement, they culled 40 items from Frogner's inventory and 3 from Kelly's. Furthermore, the committee that had formulated the pretest determined which questions measured the attitudes Rubadeau wished to measure: purism toward standard English, attitude toward linguistic or modern language theory, and attitude toward dialect.

The committee had to reach 75 to 80 percent agreement that a given question measured a particular attitude for it to be considered as a measure of that attitude. Only 3 items had to be deleted because they did not meet this requirement.

The second part of the pre- and posttest (i.e., Part II—questions 73 through 112) was made up of 40 sentences: 26 written in Black informal English; 7 written in standard informal English; and 7 written in language that would be considered as inappropriate in anyone's dialect.

The student was called upon to ascertain if a given sentence was Black informal English, standard English, or inappropriate language usage. Actually, Rubadeau was not interested in the total possible number correct (40) but only in those 26 questions which measured the student's actual knowledge of Black English. Hence, the student received a score of from 0 to 26; this score measured the student's knowledge of the dialect and not attitude toward the dialect. Therefore within this total test (Parts I and II) an instrument was created which measured both attitudes and knowledge. Pending further research, including factor analysis, the instrument will be published at a later date.

Analysis: In light of the fact that the two sections of the course came as preexisting units and that complete randomization was impossible, pretest data were submitted to analysis of variance to determine the equality of the experimental and control groups. The F-ratio of 1.34 was not significant at the .05 level and, therefore, it can be assumed that the two groups were equal.

At the completion of the experimental treatment, the *Language Inventory* was administered to all students in both the experimental and control groups; the survey was scored for the four levels of attitude and knowledge. The data were submitted to analysis of variance. The experimental treatment (the teaching of transformational grammar to illustrate the similarity between Black English and standard English)

proved to effect statistically significant differences in mean scores. In addition, it is important to note that the effects of pretesting were not statistically significant. Hence, the differences that exist between the experimental and control groups can be attributed solely to the experimental treatment and not to practice effects of testing or to the possible increased sensitization to the experimental treatment as a function of pretesting.

Reliability: *The Inventory of Language Attitudes* was analyzed for reliability. Because the inventory was scored using weighted measures, and there were no right or wrong answers for all but the section measuring the knowledge of Black English, a test-retest reliability analysis was made. Ten students in the control group had taken both the pre- and posttest and had not been exposed to the treatment condition intermediately. There was a ten-week interval between administrations of the measure. A score for each of the four measures of the inventory and the total score on the inventory for both the pre- and posttests were correlated. The Pearson Product Moment Correlation Coefficient for each pair of scores, pre- and post-, is related in Table 5. The "Method of Differences" technique was used to compute the Pearson "r" (Downie and Heath 1970, pp. 95-97).

While these reliability coefficients are certainly respectable, it should be noted that the ten-week interval between the administration of the pre- and posttests might have caused the coefficients to be unduly reduced. Indeed, the fact that the students in the control group were in a language arts methods class and were exposed to readings and discussions in the lan-

Table 5. Reliability of "Inventory of Language Attitudes"
Correlation Coefficient of Pretest and Posttest Data, Control Group

Attitude I . . . . r = .54
Attitude II . . . . r = .60
Attitude III . . . . r = .69
Knowledge of Black English . . . . r = .53
Total Inventory . . . . r = .76

guage arts during the quarter most probably affected their attitudes, though with no statistical significance.

Power: For a large effect, the power estimate for the treatment factor is approximately .94 (Cohen 1969, pp. 306-307). Also for a large effect, the power estimate for the test factor is approximately .85. In view of these power estimates, it can be concluded that the statistical analysis was most likely an accurate reflection of the effects of these two factors.

Elifson's Study

Rationale: Elifson sought to refine Rubadeau's initial investigation in two ways. First she devised a plan for achieving a design with complete randomization. Secondly, she sought to answer the question: Did Rubadeau gain significant statistical results because he talked about dialect to one group and not at all to another, or was his real treatment the demonstration of the linguistic similarity of the two dialects, as he suggested?

Design: During summer quarter 1975, a team-taught class entitled "Social Dialects and Language Learning" was conducted at Georgia State University. For twenty hours of classroom instruction all students enrolled in the class received the same instruction. The remaining twenty hours of instruction were designated as "experimental," and Rubadeau's lessons were taught to half of the class.

The students were randomly assigned to one of four groups for statistical evaluation to measure the effects of the treatment variable and to control for a pretesting factor.

At mid-quarter the class of 60 students was randomly divided into two sections and taught separately. Billiard and Elifson each participated in the instruction of both groups to eliminate a "teacher-bias." The experimental group was taught Rubadeau's lesson plans and was allowed class time to work as a group on course projects. The control group discussed classroom implementation of dialect research and was al-

lowed class time to work as a group on course projects.

The significant difference in Rubadeau's and Elifson's projects rests in the complete randomization allowed by the unique "double-class" and in the fact that Rubadeau's curriculum could be measured against another curriculum rather than against a placebo.

Hypothesis: Elifson tested the following hypothesis:

A. *Experimental hypothesis*
   Teachers enrolled in a graduate course in social dialects and engaged in a study of standard English and Black English, using transformational grammar as a tool for comparison, will develop more liberal attitudes toward language than their colleagues who are also enrolled in a graduate course in social dialects but not engaged in the comparative study.

B. *Null hypothesis*
   There will not be a significant difference in the mean scores of teacher's attitudes about language as measured by an attitude survey depending on whether the teachers did or did not study transformational grammar as a tool of comparison of the standard and Black dialects.

The Measures: Elifson used the revised *Language Inventory* developed for Rubadeau's study. She refined Rubadeau's attitude scales by submitting her pretest data to factor analysis which revealed that seven attitude factors are measured by the survey. Each item for a factor was scored "5" for the most linguistically unbiased response, as ascertained by Rubadeau. Each student was scored for seven attitude levels rather than three; each received one knowledge factor score, a scale adopted intact from Rubadeau's study.

Analysis: The data were submitted to analysis of variance which revealed no significant overall differences in attitude between the experimental and control groups, but significant differences on three specific measures were found. The experimental group showed significantly more unbiased attitudes on a measure of "Language Romanticism" (an attitude which stresses the individual nature of language), "Prescriptive Orientation to Standard English," and "Knowledge of Black English."

Further, the scores of the teachers who were both pre- and posttested were submitted to analysis of variance to determine if growth over the quarter was significant. The analysis revealed a significant growth.

Conclusion: Although the null hypothesis cannot be rejected because there was not growth over all seven measures as posited, we did find significantly greater growth in linguistic awareness on three measures among the experimental group. Additionally, both the experimental and control groups gained significantly over the twelve week quarter. The conclusion that both treatment levels were genuine treatments and that there was no "placebo" is certainly tenable. Although we cannot say that a scientific study of language is better, we can argue that it is as good as a more traditional approach to dialect. Furthermore, it produced significant gains on three measures of attitude, and the more traditional approach did not produce significant gains on any measure.

OVERALL CONCLUSION

Billiard, Rubadeau, and Elifson have shown that attitude change, as variously measured, can be effected if the attempt is made. Furthermore, it doesn't appear that there is one best way to do it. Billiard's fieldwork and the use of tapes with student teachers, Rubadeau's analytical discussion of dialects using transformational grammar, and Elifson's two treatments all effected attitude change. The job for teacher educators then seems to be commitment to the task.

References

Allen, H. B. "Attitudes of the ESL and SESD Teacher." In *Essays on Teaching English as a Second Language*

and as a Second Dialect, edited by R. P. Fox. Urbana, Ill.: National Council of Teachers of English, 1973.

Baratz, J. C. "Teaching Reading in an Urban Negro School System." In *Teaching Black Children to Read*, edited by J. C. Baratz and R. W. Shuy. Washington, D.C.: Center for Applied Linguistics, 1969.

Bereiter, C., et al. "An Academically Oriented Pre-School for Culturally Deprived Children." In *Pre-School Education Today—New Approaches to Teaching Three-, Four-, and Five-Year-Olds*, edited by F. M. Hechinger. Garden City, N.Y.: Doubleday & Co., 1966.

Campbell, D. T., and Stanley, J. C. *Experimental and Quasi-Experimental Designs for Research*. Chicago: Rand McNally & Co., 1970.

Cohen, J. *Statistical Power Analysis for the Behavioral Sciences*. New York: Academic Press, 1969.

Downie, N. M., and Heath, R. W. *Basic Statistical Methods*. 3rd ed. New York: Harper & Row, 1970.

Festinger, L. *A Theory of Cognitive Dissonance*. Stanford, Calif.: Stanford University Press (1957), 1966.

Frogner, E. *The Language Inquiry*. Edwardsville, Ill.: U.S. Department of Health, Education, and Welfare, U.S. Office of Education Project Number HE-145, 1969.

Glass, G. V., and Stanley, J. C. *Statistical Methods in Education and Psychology*. Englewood Cliffs, N.J.: Prentice-Hall, 1970.

Golden, R. I. *Effectiveness of Instructional Tapes for Changing Regional Speech Patterns*. Detroit: Detroit Public Schools, 1962.

Hurst, C. G., Jr. *Psychological Correlates in Dialectolalia*. Washington, D.C.: Howard University Communication Science Research Center, 1965.

Kirk, R. E. *Experimental Design*. Belmont, Calif. Brooks/Cole Publishing Co., 1968.

Kurath, H. *Handbook of the Linguistic Geography of New England*. Providence, R.I.: Brown University Press, 1939.

Labov, W. "Academic Ignorance and Black Intelligence." *Atlantic* 229, no. 6 (June 1972): 59-67.

Lin, S. C. *Pattern Practice in the Teaching of Standard English to Students with a Nonstandard Dialect*. New York: Teachers College, Columbia University, 1965.

Mantell, A. L. "An Assessment of Two Curriculum Strategies for Increasing Bidialectal Proficiency of Speakers of Non-Standard Dialect in Fifth Grade in the New York Metropolitan Area." Ph.D. dissertation, New York University, 1973.

McDavid, R. I. "A Checklist of Significant Features for Discriminating Social Dialect." In *Dimensions of Dialect,* edited by E. L. Everetts. Urbana, Ill.: National Council of Teachers of English, 1967.

McDavid, R. I. "Field Procedures: Instructions for Investigators, Linguistic Atlas of the Gulf States." In *A Manual for Dialect Research in the Southern States,* edited by L. Pederson, et al. University, Ala.: University of Alabama Press, 1974.

Ney, J. W. "Predator or Pedagogue? The Teacher of the Bilingual Child." *The English Record* 21, no. 4 (1971): 12-19.

O'Neil, W. "Paul Roberts' Rules of Order: The Misuse of Linguistics in the Classroom." *The Urban Review* 2, no. 7 (1968): 12-17.

Pederson, L., et al. *A Manual for Dialect Research in the Southern States.* University, Ala.: University of Alabama Press, 1974.

Plaister, J. *Audiolingual Methods in the Language Arts Program.* Urbana, Ill.: National Council of Teachers of English, 1967.

Rafferty, M. San Diego *Union,* September 10, 1967. Quoted in Shuy, R. W., "Bonnie and Clyde Tactics in English Teaching." *Contemporary English: Change and Variation,* edited by D. L. Shores, pp. 278-288. New York: J. P. Lippincott, 1972.

Shuy, R. W. "Bonnie and Clyde Tactics in English Teaching." In *Contemporary English: Change and Variation,* edited by D. L. Shores, pp. 278-288. New York: J. P. Lippincott, 1972.

Sledd, J. "Bi-Dialectalism: The Linguistics of White Supremacy." *English Journal* 58 (1969): 1307-1315.

Stewart, W. A. "Sociolinguistic Factors in the History of American Negro Dialects." *Florida FL Reporter* 5, no. 2 (1967).

Zale, E. M. "The Case Against Bi-Dialectalism." Paper presented at the sixth annual Teaching English as a Second Language Convention, February 28, 1972, Washington, D.C.

Michele Rubin

When Is Gladys Knight and the Pips Arts-in-Education?
or
Children Teach the Teacher How to Teach

When the artist makes contact with a child's inner space and finds Gladys Knight and the Pips living there, that is where new learning will start. The artist's full acceptance of the place of Gladys Knight and the Pips in the child's life comes early in the "Arts-in-Education" process. What comes next is an exploration of the nooks and crannies of the child's self, with plays, poems, stories, and drawings documenting the adventure.

Plays with titles like: *The Drunk Man and the Police, The Gossipy Women, Beware of Strangers, Why Is Anthony Late?, The Sly Stones,* and *The Shoeshine Dope Peddler.*

Writing with revelations, such as:

> *"She talked as if*
> *A fly was in her mouth*
> *Trying to get out."*

and

> *"She is quiet*
> *As a pillow*
> *On a*
> *Comfortable bed."*

Writing that releases anger, as in:

> *"I feel like*
> *I want to*
> *Kill somebody*
> *And*
> *Shoot someone*
> *And*
> *Cut someone inside."*

And writing such as:

> *"I want to be*
> *A black cat,*
> *With*
> *Black soft fur*
> *Green eyes*
> *That glow in the dark*
> *At night.*
> *And people see me."*

For five years, three Atlanta institutions have worked together in a revolutionary program in education.

Through the combined efforts of the Atlanta Public Schools, Clark College, and the Academy Theatre, Atlanta school children have come in active, direct, and regular contact with professional theatre artists and with college students who are in training in the use of the arts in working with children.

A series of courses provides prospective teachers with experience in:

1. Exercising and developing their own creative potential;

2. Dealing openly and constructively with others in groups;

3. Relating to children in situations freed from traditional teacher-student roles;

4. Using the arts as teaching strategies; and

5. Recognizing, accepting, and cultivating individual differences in physically and emotionally involving learning activities.

The courses are:

Creative Arts in which college students first discover and explore their own potential in the creative arts; then, in small groups, design experiences for children, using the creative arts to further the children's interest and/or knowledge in material they are studying; and finally, carry out their plans in elementary school classrooms.

Play Creating in which a group of college students create, through improvisation, a play for children. They then perform the play in elementary schools in the area.

Real World Work in which advanced students receive academic credit for working in the schools, leading groups of children in improvisational drama and creative writing activities.

For six years, as director of the program, I have worked primarily in the Black community. I will delineate my observations of culture-based characteristics unique to Blacks, and discuss how these characteristics can be used to develop learning activities suitable to children in that culture. The **process,** however, is applicable to any culture.

I will also give examples of activities designed to draw out culture-based characteristics of people of any culture. Those characteristics can then inform the teacher how to design learning activities for the classroom suitable to the learning style of the students.

My work with children is in improvisational drama and in creative writing. As an artist/ teacher, it is my intention to delve with the children into their individual perceptions and feelings and to provide them with the technical assistance to express their perceptions and feelings within the framework of an artistic discipline. The very nature of my work with people brings forth their core personalities.

I have worked with people of all ages, in rural, urban, suburban, and small town settings; with people rich and poor, and from all levels of educational background. At their core, people all have the same hopes, fears, and needs, but different groups of people express their hopes, fears, and needs in different ways. The differences occur as a function of each group's particular culture.

The Black inner-city children I work with grow in a full, rich, vigorous, warm environment that is a total culture in all senses of the word. It is a culture different from, but no less than, White mainstream American culture.

Black children are often taught as if they were stunted, deprived, deficient, and "wrong" because they do not connect with White mainstream American culture. In school they are, for the most part, taught by teachers who speak from and promote White middle socioeconomic status (SES) values. Sometimes these are White teachers. Sometimes these are Black teachers who, as members of the mainstream middle SES, believe in promoting the values and language of that culture and have turned their backs on their own origins.

My thesis is that Black children will learn better when their teachers are aware of and fully accept the fact that their students grow in a flourishing and valid culture which is due recognition and respect. Some characteristics of this culture appear in children as they function as individuals, and some characteristics appear in group behavior.

To me, the most striking characteristic of all of the people with whom I work is the total integration of their response to anything and everything around them. Every limb of the body, each sound or word uttered, reveals a person functioning with total unity. It is never unclear to me what one of my students is feeling. If it is anger, fists flail, curses fly, nostrils flare, and energy boils through the body. If it is joy, a hand slaps a thigh and laughter curves the body with a rush of sound. The feeling may be of conflict and confusion, but when it is, words and body speak together to convey a picture of one totally immersed in confusion.

Responses are intense, which adds emphasis to the unity of response. I work with people who have deeply felt responses, and who express their feelings with intensity. Even if the response is one of coolness, there is nothing quite so clear, so subtle, or quite so definite as being tuned out by one of my fourth grade students.

The children are physical with each other. In fighting, playing, walking, talking, singing—whatever the activity—there is a great deal of easy, comfortable physical contact. A lot of the physical contact comes through fighting. Among the children, fighting is the first, often the only, option seen for solving problems. Violence and death are an everyday part of life—on a firsthand basis.

But physicality pervades other interactions too. The children lean on each other, drape themselves about the others, lay hands on the other in conversation, and, in general, use physical contact as a natural part of their relationship with others.

The only time I have seen any anxiety about having physical contact is at about the fourth grade level when boys' and girls' attention turns to the other in a new way, and when one may not be especially interested in the physical attentions of the other—at least in public. But even the physically awkward boy-girl period comes early and seems short. Soon an easily accepted physicality takes place as part of the coupling process which is seen early as being proper, good, and desirable.

The children are spontaneous. In almost all adult groups, and in many groups of children, intense stimulation and motivation must be provided to provoke a creative response. Here, after an initial icebreaking, trust-building period, only very slight stimulation is needed to provoke creative responses. As a matter of fact, response is so spontaneous and so intense and complete that channeling and disciplining responses become the only problem. The children respond instantaneously and fully in their personal interactions; for instance, fights used to start and finish before I would even know the first insult had been hurled. This spontaneity is a part of a pattern in creative response also.

Everything about these children bespeaks style. In dress, movement, dance, language, and music, there is great concern for and sensitivity to style and beauty. What one says may be interesting, but how one says it can be fine. To walk down a hall is okay, but to walk as if boss lets everyone know you are there—and won't take nothing off of nobody! Blue jeans are al-right, but if embroidered with your astrological sign and worn with a blue jean beret and four-inch denim platforms, they are "bad."

Which brings us to language. The children I work with are described as lacking in verbal skills. I have never encountered children who speak with more verbal skill. The children are poets. Their culture has instilled in them a love of a good story, the embellished piece of grapevine gossip, the perfect metaphor—even the perfect insult. It has instilled a sense of the rhythmic, movement and musical possibilities of the spoken word. It has made an unusually large number of its members into storytellers who, in their storytelling, improvise, and respond to and build on their audiences' responses. They use dialogue in their storytelling—dialogue in which excellent mimicry occurs. They direct questions to their audiences and incorporate the answers in the story. They use gesture and body language, and supply vivid detail and sound effects. The good rap goes on and on. The point is not the point. The telling of it is what counts. No matter if there is no end. Did you enjoy the telling with me?

The language is definitely not standard English. I believe the teaching of standard English to be essential. But only when taught as a second language—a language useful as a tool to get ahead in the world. There is simply no need to attempt to destroy the beautiful, flowing, richly poetic language called Black English. Luckily, as long as there are streets, the language will stay alive. I see much unnecessary conflict set up in children who have been told how bad their natural language is.

Several expressions of culture as it appears in individual children have been mentioned, including:

• a unity and integration of response;
• an intensity of feeling in response;
• an easy physicality with others;
• spontaneity;
• concern with style in all aspects of living, especially in dress, movement, and language.

There is also group behavior which I observe to be an expression of training within the culture. Again, I make distinctions between what are expressions of human characteristics, and what are expressions of a particular culture. The characteristics I mention here are unique to Blacks with whom I have worked, but are not unique to inner-city Blacks. They occur in rural Black settings also.

The situations in which I have been able to observe group behavior which is cultural in origin are:

- improvisational drama classes and performances of plays for audiences;
- free play in the schoolyard, gym, and halls;
- classrooms.

Several different types of performances occur: performances by college students for children and performances by children for children and adults.

Most of the performing that the children do is in our classroom in the elementary school. A cloakroom at one end provides a backstage area, with stage right and left entrances. A combination of movable desks and carpeting form the seating area at the other end of the room. Children from other classes are invited to attend performances. Audiences range in size from ten to fifty.

In performance I see marked and immediately evident characteristics in the relationship between the players and the audience. The audience arrives in the room ready to participate in, not to witness, an event. From the moment of entry, audience members comment on setting, props, try to interact with actors who are on stage, and begin urging the beginning of the action. They are, in fact, the action.

Once the play begins, the audience becomes an active force in the playing out of the drama. The plays are pre-set in terms of what events will happen and in what order. But the dialogue is slightly different each time, allowing for improvisation within a set framework. Audience actions often spark freer improvisation. Audience members are highly vocal in their participation in the plays. They hoot and holler and take sides during fight scenes, shouting encouragement to their favorites, and often need to be restrained from joining in to help. They loudly whisper encouragement and suggestions when a sympathetic character is in trouble, and give a round of "right-ons" when he or she does well. They sing and clap along with any music or chants that occur in the play, and as best they can, dance in their chairs until they can restrain themselves no longer, and then jump to their feet to dance along. The audience has a strong effect on the players. I have seen child actors waken to the fact that they have the audience going and string out a two-line speech into a lengthy scene with the audience spurring them on.

There is a kind of theatre that strives to achieve participation of the audience in the dramatic action of the play. But, in my experience, having the audience on their own become a participant in the dramatic events is a phenomenon unique to Black audiences.

James V. Hatch, in an article in the Black theatre issue of *The Drama Review* (1972), quotes Professor Thomas Pawley of Lincoln University regarding observations of behavior patterns of Black audiences:

. . . shouting, jeering, hooting, laughter and an infinite number of non-linguistic vocal reactions indicative of approval or disapproval, enjoyment or dissatisfaction. Physical responses include beating on the seats, stamping on the floor, nudging or kicking companies, clapping or slapping hands (give me some skin), rocking back and forth, and in extreme instances, leaping to one's feet in the manner of a sports crowd.

Swearing, especially if it involves the "dozens," sexual references, both overt and covert, sharp repartee, and "flams," will undoubtedly produce whoops of delight. Scenes of violence and physical conflict will also arouse the audience. . . . (p. 21)

Pawley suggests that the Black audience response has at least five traceable influences:

1. The Black church and the congregation's participation;

2. The Black night-club experience;

3. The Black stage performances at theatres like the Apollo in Harlem, the Howard in Washington, D.C., and the Regal in Chicago;

4. Sports performances, particularly those based on feats of Black athletes competing with Whites, e.g., Jackie Robinson and Joe Louis;

5. The origin of it all, the African audience tradition. (p. 22)

He quotes a report of a Nigerian audience response to a performance:

Between explosions of laughter, spectators offered a constant stream of suggestion, instant criticism, and jokes of their own as Ladipo's company continued its performance. Surprisingly, the injections and other symptoms of the Yoruba affinity for anarchy did not seem to hamper the players who were able to build much of the by-play into their production. (p. 22)

Pawley's observations of adult Black audiences' response patterns match my observations of young Black audiences. The games and play of the children I work with reveal more traits. Beyond qualities evident in all children's games (repetition, simple rhyme, and rhythm patterns), the following are some qualities I have observed as being special to the games of Black children.

- Rhythmic patterns are often fairly complex.
- There is a great deal of and a great variety of body movement.
- Intonation has great variety, a wide range, and a rich combination of sounds ("Hanky in a Pocket" as compared to "Tisket-a-Tasket").
- A call and response pattern occurs.
- There is, built into many games, room for personal style to show in improvisation (as in "Aunt Dinah's Dead," and "Zoodio").
- There is an immediacy to everyday life in the content of the games. (Aunt Dinah "lives in the country," but she's "gonna move to town." When she gets there, she's "gonna shake, shake, shake, 'til the sun goes down.")

I have touched on only a few areas in which I believe Black children are trained within their culture. I have not even mentioned special sets of priorities; sets of priorities that put seeing Aunt Rubye, whom you haven't seen for six months, as being more important than getting to class exactly at 9:00 a.m.; priorities that put letting the custodian sing all he wants and as loudly as he wants, above having quiet in the halls; priorities that make a principal see that a hungry child gets a free lunch someway, somehow. Also, I have not yet mentioned training in acceptance of the humanness that exists in us all. The culture is one that teaches a valuing and accepting of a multitude of differences in its people. A short story written by a first grader says it better than I can:

HEYMAN THE MONSTER

Once upon a time somebody threw a yellow hat on his head. He has had a wedding veil on his head also. He said he is going to a wedding. Herman is a dumb man. Herman is a sissy and a crazy monster. Herman always makes mistakes, but he is human.

Often, teachers ignore an entire set of cultural characteristics in their students. They teach from the point of view of their own culture or from whatever culture they believe it desirable to belong to. To say that this creates a communication gap is an understatement. At its extreme, it is the same as sending unprepared children to a foreign country for their education—or bringing in foreign missionaries who are convinced that they need to educate the natives to the path of righteousness. Teachers need to see their students with unclouded eyes. They need to learn from the students. The first thing they need to see and learn is just exactly who the students are. They need to see their students without judging them—without comparing students' behavior and modes of expression to their own or to someone else's definition of desirable behavior.

For teachers to begin to see their students without judging them may mean observing the students while not interacting with them. It is hard to begin the process of nonjudgmental observation while trying to keep a classroom functioning smoothly. It is easier to drop judgment while observing children in free play in the schoolyard, in the halls after school, at the carnival, at the dance.

No matter what the culture of the children—Black, White, Chicano—the children will begin to reveal to the teacher what she or he needs to do, so that the children will learn better in the classroom.

The Black children I work with reveal the characteristics I have discussed. They are spontaneous; physical; have intense feeling; are concerned with style, especially in language; and are integrated in their responses and reactions. No wonder these children have trouble learning through usual teaching methods and materials. The usual methods require them to fragment themselves; to separate their feelings from what they are to learn; to sit quietly instead of being physically and emotionally involved in the learning process; to reject as bad the vivid language and imagery with which they are familiar in favor of a foreign tongue (standard English) which they are not even told will be a new language to them; to forget about Aunt Dinah "shake, shake, shakin' 'til the sun goes down," and "Sally, walkin' through the alley," in favor of Jane (do they even know anyone named Jane?) walking her new Dalmatian puppy, Spot, down some suburban sidewalk.

We need to integrate learning methods and materials with the lives and cultures of the children we teach. This means allowing learning to occur as it now does outside of school, through physical and emotional involvement in the material to be learned. This means excitement and sometimes noise. For children who speak nonstandard English, this may mean allowing them to master the skill of reading with materials written in their own language. If only insufficient materials are available, let them write their own materials. Teach standard English as a second language after they learn the skill of reading in their own language.

Whatever the culture of the children, it has implications in the cognitive learning process. It is for us to see the children clearly to get the information necessary to begin to find the teaching methods and materials which will make it possible for them to learn.

My particular work has allowed me to learn about a culture other than my own. As an "outsider" to the Black culture, it is easy for me to see characteristics unique to that culture. Just as I take for granted and see no particular value in cultural characteristics that I live each day in my fairly middle SES White life, members of the Black culture often fail to recognize and value qualities of their own culture. I see this to be markedly true of some Blacks who have "made it" in mainstream America.

I see it as being particularly important for members of the Black community who are working with Black children to become aware of the value of the characteristics of their culture. After all, if I criticize a Black child's ways because they are dissimilar from my own, I can always be dismissed as being White. But what happens when a Black teacher criticizes the Black child for qualities inherent in the child's culture? I think that creates considerable conflict and confusion: If a teacher who is Black thinks Black is bad, then maybe there is something to the idea that Black is bad. While I do not doubt the good intentions of those members of the Black community who use this tactic to "improve" its members, I think it is the origin of the self-hatred I see in some Black children.

I believe we can discover and accept and use the qualities of any culture to further learning by the children within that culture. Then, standing firmly and proudly as a member of his or her own culture, a child can be taught about qualities of another culture, and even the language of another culture, as necessary tools to achieving within that other culture, if that is what the child wants to do.

My work in creative writing and improvisational drama has proved extremely valuable in discovering characteristics of a culture other than my own. I will share with you some examples and suggestions for activities that I have found useful. All of the examples in this chapter are from students of the E. A. Ware Public School in Atlanta.

First, the following guidelines contain the elements that go into making an activity successful in terms of drawing out and giving value to the participants' unique individual and cultural characteristics.

- The leader must provide the focus, the stimulation for the activity.
- There must be enough structure provided to prevent chaos, but not so much structure that the creativity of the participants is stifled.
- There must be an insistence that each individual is capable of and has the right to give his or her own response—whatever it may be. (My only exemptions to this are that the children may not damage people or property through their responses.)
- In group activities, there must be an insistence that those in the group accept the creative response of each individual and work off that.

For stimulating creative writing, I sometimes start with group stories. To start, a couple of nonspecific objects are placed together in the center of the table. Objects have included an empty three-pound coffee can covered in aluminum foil, with several sheets of crinkled pink tissue paper billowing out of it; a large, cloudy plastic globe, nested in a bed of lime green tissue paper; and 25 feet of electric-blue, four-inch flexible tubing twisted and balled up in itself.

Each child has a piece of paper and pencil. Each child writes the first sentence of a story, making sure to identify the object as whatever he or she thinks it is (an octopus, a magic ball, an oil tank). The papers are then all passed, in any orderly manner, to other children, who silently read the first sentence and add a second. Papers are passed again with children now reading two sentences and adding a third. This is continued until enough has been added to build a whole story. Warning needs to be given when the end is drawing near, so that children can draw their stories to a close.

Here are two group stories:

THE GLOBE THAT LEARNED HOW TO PLAY

There was once a globe that never could turn. But one day it fell and the wind hit it. It spinned around like a flying moon. Then it was bragging about how it could fly with the wind. And it could. It danced and spun and sailed, and made music all the while. Children liked to play on it.

Later the globe became friends to all the people who like him. He played and played until he died. When he died he had all his friends at his funeral. They all took flowers.

THE ENORMOUS BILL

A octopus was in bed wishing his wife would come back. He started crying because he was lonely. He cried and cried and his tears covered the floor. The carpet got all wet. He cried so much that the room begin to look like a swimming pool. He busted the window and the water came running out so fast. He went to somebody home. Then he called a plumber. The plumber could not stop the water. The plumber left and said, "I will send you your great enormous bill."

Sometimes groupings of nonspecific objects are used to touch off individual stories also.

THE LONG-NECKED MONSTER
by Charlayne Venson

Once upon a time in a faraway village a ugly long-necked monster landed from nowhere and all the people ran with fright. The dogs and cats started barking and meowing and all the little children started crying. The ugly monster with his red glowing eyes and all those ridges blowed fire out of his mouth. He had two heads and nine pairs of arms and two pairs of feet.

All the people stopped running and looked at one another and said, "Why are we running? He haven't did us any harm."

And the monster went back where he came from.

This fantasy was started by the phrase: If I had a million dollars . . . .

by Angela Williams

If I had a million dollars I would buy me a El-dorado. I would like to take a trip to New York, California, New Jersey. I would have servants to bring my food and to go get my children. I would have a car for my daughter and a car for me and my husband. I would have a police to stand out and guard. I would have two of them to be in the house because I do not want to be threaten. That is what I am going to do with my money.

One day some of the children "became" statues. The others wrote about what they thought the statues were doing.

by Richard Julian

Two ladies are fighting in the street. The police came to the scene and stopped the fight. The ladies didn't like it so they began fighting the policemen. They finally stopped. They were sent to territorial prison for police abuse.

by Andrea Ford

She is a wino from a broken home. Ever since she was a child her parents broke up so she went out into the world. She comes to our school to eat. She is retarded. She went to a psychiatrist but they could not help her.

One day in a subway a nice man saw her and was concerned. He took her home, and now she is okay.

by Edward Birt

A lady witness a murder and call the police. The murder was on Whitehall Street. The man was 5 feet tall, had brown eyes and brown complexion. The man shot the man 3 times.

by Ellen Matthews

Old mother hubbard lives in the shoe and has so many children that she don't know what to do. Her boy friend is going to take her to a movie so she puts on her wool hat and her colorful scarf with her black glasses and black fur coat.

I think she is old and for the first time her boy friend is going to take her out some where. She is very happy. A baby sitter is keeping her children.

When her boy friend came and got her he saw all of her children and he shot out of the house. He was a nervous wreck, Mother hubbard was so sad, so she live happily ever after.

Once, children were told that they could, for an hour, become anything else in the world that they wanted to be, and could write about their new selves. Here is what some of them said.

I AM A SUN
by Lloyd McKibbins

When I wake up in the morning I let everybody know. I let my sun up and my heat out. I get tired up there by myself. I can see every where. I even let my sun shine thousand and thousands of miles away. I can even see in Arizona. I shine my sun on many people. And I am nice.

I AM SMOKE
by Clarence Colbert

I am some smoke
That's coming out out of a train.
I can fly all over town.

One spring day a group went outside and wrote love letters to newly green plants. Letters such as:

Dear Vine,
    I wish you were a human being so we could talk to each other. You twist all over the fence. I love to watch. You are so sweet I wish I was like you. Because you never get in trouble.

Your Love,
Sheryl Hicks

P.S. Write me back some times. Don't forget I still love you very very much. My children are waiting to see you. Every day when I walk into my house they say, "Mommy when will the vine come?"

On election day, students presented their platforms and held a small mock election on the basis of the platforms.

by Angela Jones

If I were govenor of Georgia I would make sure that food prices go down. I will be the nicest govenor Georgia ever had. I will make sure people use the peace sign wisely. I will throw every bottle of liquor away, and burn bad drugs.

One day I read a story based on a dream a schoolchild had, and invited students to write down one of their own dreams.

NIGHT DREAMS
by Tyron Nelson

A witch.
A snake.
I dreamed about Heyman the monster.
I dreamed about Dracula.
I dreamed about wrestling.
And I dreamed about a policeman got killed.
And I dreamed about a wreck yesterday.
And I dreamed he went into the teacher's room.
And fell out the window.
I dreamed about the ambulance came.
And I saw a man rob a bank.
I dreamed about I was scared.
And I dreamed about I was a cowboy.

After the children had been meeting for a while, they began to write directly about their own feelings. On a cold, wet fall day, we wrote about the weather and how it made us feel.

by Tony Zeigler

Blue, yellow
Degrees, 30.
I feel good.
I would like to eat pigs' feet at home.

The assignment to write about what it feels like to be angry brought a lot of response.

by Angela Jones

Sometimes I feel so angry that I could
Rip up my dog's sweater
Throw him out the window
And toss him in the ocean.
I feel so angry
I could squeeze toothpaste
In my mother's turnip greens.

Some other feelings:

RIGHT NOW I FEEL VERY EXCITED
by Lloyd McKibbins

I am more excited than my whole class.
I am excited as a bunch of bees
That have some honey in a nest.
I am very excited today
Because we are having our annual carnival.
I feel so excited
That I can jump into the wall.
And I am so excited
That I can jump over the world.
And I can't wait to
Ride the bumper cars and
Taste the pickles.

JOY
by Lisa McFadden

My heart is pounding so hard with joy
That I can lay down and go to sleep.
My lungs are dancing inside of me.
My tonsils are singing.
My brains are going fast asleep.

And finally, some comments about love:

LOVE
by Tempist Spikes

Love is something that's real serious. Watch out, for it can get you, right or wrong.

If I would get married I would not go with another man, because some men can be jealous of the other man. And you can get hurt from your man.

And sometimes your man can be going to another woman, and you can get jealous.

SINCE I FELL FOR YOU
by Angela Brown

I feel about love. A boy will make me happy, because a boy will make me feel good inside. I just like some boys but none of them is in my room. I have some of them over my aunt's house.

One named Terry, one Michael. But Michael do not know that I go with Terry, and Terry do not know that I go with Michael. I hope they will not find out.

I just love that record about "Since I fell for you". He took my love and he's gone.

One creative writing project involved pairing first graders with fifth graders who had been writing for a while. Each fifth grader read to the first grader from stories and poems that the older children had published in a booklet. Then the fifth grader invited the younger child to tell a story. The fifth grader wrote down the first grader's story as it was told. Sometimes pictures were also drawn. College students typed the stories and organized them with the pictures into booklets which were then distributed. This provided an excellent learning experience for all, an experience in which the fifth graders provided their own work as models.

One story written in such a manner follows:

THE MONSTER AND THE STOLEN GIRL
story by Michelle Smith
written down by Tammy Key

The little girl was in her bed asleep. The monster came in and got her. He went to the forest and laid her down and then he chopped her up. Then he ate her up. He went to sit down to get him some rest. He went and got him another meal. He went back to the woods to sit down and the little girl's mother came looking for her. The monster got her and ate her up, too.

The children who wrote the above material range from first to fifth grade. They were not specially selected in any way. Some are good students, some are "discipline problems," many are special education students. All of them were free to drop out of the creative writing groups at any time. None did.

To give examples of the plays produced through improvisational drama is difficult. The titles given earlier suggest the flavor of the work. A description of plays from one class on one day may provide further insight into the kind of information this work gives the teacher.

The day was Halloween. The children had been working for several months, so they needed no special activities to stimulate them to creative production of plays. All that was needed was a focal point for their energies and the structure within which to produce. The class was split up into five groups. Each group was directed to do a play about Halloween.

The plays that resulted were:

Trick or Treat, in which the man of the house steals the trick-or-treaters' candy.

The Trick or Treat Party, in which Dracula and Frankenstein come to the door and frighten the children.

Trick or Drink, in which the trick-or-treaters ask for water, but are given gin instead.

Trick-or-Treaters on Trick or Treating Night, in which a man puts poison in an apple and gives the apple to the children, whereupon he is arrested by the police.

The End of Trick or Treat, in which a child is given yet another poisoned apple. The child dies in her mother's arms, and the trick or treat tradition dies with her.

Techniques for leading improvisational drama groups are so plentiful that they would easily fill a book. Often, with children, all that is necessary is focus and structure (as in the instructions for the Halloween plays).

Another simple method within small groups is to have each child decide what role he or she wants to play (police officer, robber, mother, teacher). Then, the children in each group decide what kind of setting or situation would bring all of these people together. (For example, a child's mother is having a conference with the teacher in the office when the robber comes in to steal the carnival funds. The school police officer is alerted, and the chase begins.)

Some work can be done in pairs, with the teacher assigning roles. Children can mill about the room and at a signal (a hand clap, a shake of a tambourine) each must find a partner. The taller person in each pair is to pretend to be a police officer giving out a speeding ticket. The shorter person in each pair is the motorist, trying to convince the police officer that he or she was not speeding. The pairs interact simultaneously, and the result for each pair is determined solely by the two people involved.

The same structure can be used for groups of more than two. For example, in threes, the person with the brightest clothes is the teacher, trying to determine which of the other two started the fight.

The possibilities are endless. To be successful, however, activities must take place according to the guidelines mentioned earlier. That is, there must be structure and focus, and there must be complete respect for and acceptance of each individual's creative response (so long as the creative response does not involve damaging people or property).

The examples and descriptions of the children's work make clear that they do not live in a Dick, Jane, and Spot world. I don't know any children who do.

Recently, I brought a group of children to a conference to perform a play designed to reveal characteristics of the Black urban child's culture. Afterwards, the children participated in discussion and workshop activities with the adults attending the conference to create learning activities based on what had just been observed. Later, many adults expressed amazement at the children's sophistication, verbal skill, and confidence and ease with themselves in the potentially threatening conference setting. It was, by the way, a conference for educators.

Those educators were put in a situation where they were invited to focus on the revelations that the children made about themselves. The educators used their own observations to structure activities suitable to the children's learning style. The adults saw some children learn how to count by odd numbers, others learn how to spell some tricky words, and others recognize and tell something about famous Black Americans. The children did indeed teach the teachers how to teach.

The process is simple. It involves nonjudgmental observation of children, identification of existing cultural characteristics, and application of these characteristics to classroom material. The rewards are excitement, involvement, and learning.

Reference

Hatch, J. V. "A Guide to 200 Years of Drama," Black Theatre Issue, T-56. *The Drama Review* 16, no. 4 (December 1972).

Child Development Research with Inner-City Children

Two factors which have been previously identified as contributing to the school failure of inner-city children are the children's supposed negative self-esteem and their supposed relative inability to intellectually process abstract information. The first two chapters in this section review research on these topics and describe methodological flaws in the research which led to these positions. In addition, the chapters describe the philosophical orientation of cultural deficiency which influenced the selection of variables chosen for study and the interpretation of data obtained.

Sadie Grimmett reviews studies addressing the linguistic and memory capabilities of inner-city Black children. Following an analysis of the relationship between language and memory, she describes her own work which suggests that the infor-

mation processing capabilities of inner-city children are not deficient when compared to non-inner-city counterparts. Among the many cogent points that Grimmett makes are her argument for a conception of the capabilities of inner-city children in a nonracial framework and her discussion of the heterogeneity of inner-city children.

Valora Washington similarly reviews the theoretical framework and research involving the learning of racial identity. Too often the deficit paradigm has focused research on the inner-city family as the hypothesized cause of all the problems of inner-city children. We feel that a major contribution by Washington is her thorough description of variables, other than parent behavior, which potentially influence racial identification.

Harvey Moore presents an empirical investigation of racial differences in self-derogation and student identification of significant others. His findings, which were based on high school students, contribute to a growing body of literature contradictory to the conventional wisdom that inner-city Black children compared to White counterparts lack feelings of self-worth. Moore reports a nonsignificant difference in self-derogation between the two racial groups studied. Further, Moore discusses those persons identified as significant others by the Black and White students. The lack of identification of school personnel as significant others by the Black students is notable. The generalizability of these findings to younger children naturally requires replication using younger children as subjects. However, Moore's data illustrate, as do Grimmett's, that studies which do not confound socioeconomic status and race obtain results contrary to the large body of previous literature where such confounding occurred.

The final chapter in this section is perhaps most relevant to persons involved in theory construction and research work.

John Dill discusses limitations of current research work and examines in brief the existing major development theories. Following this analysis of the status quo, Dill offers a set of basic premises upon which to develop a theory of development of inner-city children. We question whether a theory based upon Dill's premises would apply only to inner-city children. Rather, we feel that the strength of Dill's chapter is the identification of principles and complex variables that should influence the direction of research and theorizing concerning inner-city and non-inner-city children alike. It is now recognized that univariate analyses of child behavior are extremely limited in their ability to explain and predict complex child behavior. Dill's conception of matrices of variables is consistent with the positions of other research workers arguing for ecological or multivariate methodologies. It is becoming apparent that only through such studies and theory development will the child development field begin to understand the interaction of the many forces that shape a child's development.

Sadie A. Grimmett

Information Processing Competencies of Inner-City Black Children: Knowing How to Know the World

The decade of the 1960s was marked by special attention to the poor as a specific educational group (Bloom, Davis, and Hess 1965; Passow 1963; Reissman 1962). Poor children were found to be failing in school in large numbers, thus the emphases were on accounting for poor children's failure in school and how best to reverse it (C. Deutsch 1965). The planning and implementing of programs and projects to reverse the poor child's failure has come to be known as compensatory education for which the promise of success was high in those early years. Now, after some ten years experience with these programs, there is little optimism for compensatory efforts. It is generally conceded that compensatory education has not, on a large scale, achieved its aim (Jensen 1969; Winschel 1970). The current period seems to be marked by rethinking and reevaluating beliefs about the poor and the programs for the poor derived from these beliefs.

The topic *Demythologizing the Inner-City Child* implies that some fictional ideas have entered

our knowledge about inner-city children and that we need to reexamine our knowledge in order to distinguish that which is valid from that which is invalid. In my opinion, the bases of compensatory education have been irrelevant to the cognitive development of inner-city Black children. Compensatory education has seemingly been formulated on assumptions of differences between Blacks and Whites in ways of thinking and of alikeness in poor Black children for degree and kind of thinking. The claim to be made here is that race is not an effective classification when considering basic ways of processing information. For the successful education of inner-city Black children I wish to suggest that ways of information processing be viewed developmentally or according to theoretical constructs about processing information. Some rather recent data on basic cognitive processing of information by poor Black children in their early years of schooling will be presented in this chapter. The indexes of basic information processing will be language and memory, with the focus on how these recent findings relate to the deficit and different hypotheses that dominate current accounts of Black children's learning and on what implications language and memory results have for reformulating views about Black children's capabilities. It is a premise of this discussion that reconceptualization of poor Black children's basic cognitive functioning will have import for the kinds of compensatory education developed for children.

LANGUAGE AND THINKING

Processing of information permits children to know, operate on, and control their world. To know the world in increasingly complex ways, an important task for all children is to attain basic skills that facilitate the acquisition, storage, and retrieval of information.

One important basic skill for knowing the world is language, for language is one means of operating on the environment (Bruner, Oliver, and Greenfield 1966; Bever 1970; Ervin-Tripp 1973). For example, when a very young child plays with a pet, perhaps a dog, the parent talks about the pet— "It is a dog; it has paws; it has fur," and so on. The child learns these terms and attaches them to the animal and its attributes. The child is developing implicit meaning structures—the child's dictionary according to McNeill (1970)—that facilitate interpretation of events and permit ultimately indirect manipulation of events. When the child in our example is told that grandmother has a dog, although the child has not seen the dog, he or she can interpret, bring meaning to, the statement. Additionally, through play and talk with the parents, the child learns other characteristics of dogs. Perhaps the child has learned that dogs are likely to bite if their tails are pulled. When approaching a dog, the child thinks about this information and uses it. The child is becoming less dependent upon direct experience for knowing. Intuitively we can agree with Piaget's view (Morehead and Morehead 1974) that being able to "think about" something decreases reliance upon immediate experience. Language is one cognitive function that enables us to be removed from experiences which by mental representation can enhance flexibility in handling occurring environmental data.

Given the importance of language for processing information, it is understandable that as the concern for educating poor Black children increased so did attention to Black children's language.

LANGUAGE AND THE DEFICIT HYPOTHESIS

The empirical evidence collected on Black children was interpreted as indicating language deficits (John and Goldstein 1964). Black children's language was considered dysfunctional for thinking and communicating (Bereiter and Englemann 1966) and hence a hindrance to the intellectual development fostered in the classroom. This dysfunction was attributed to the children's environment which was characterized as lacking the stimulation of syntax and

semantics comparable to the middle socio-economic status (SES) environment (M. Deutsch 1965).

Having so conceptualized Black children's language, compensatory efforts were directed, usually, to the teaching of language (Bereiter and Englemann 1966; Blank and Solomon 1969). Instruction centered on correct articulation, labeling, and simple sentence constructions as the necessary ingredients to alleviate Black children's language deficiencies as determined from speech (e.g., -ed, -ing). Seldom was it considered whether these omissions were in common with other children's omissions and thus might be a function of development. An inference from recent evidence is that the language omissions by poor Black children do not differ much from omissions by Anglo children. As demonstrated on the sentence repetition task, poor Black children include critical markers (e.g., so, that, where, because, etc.) as often as their Anglo counterparts (Anastasiow and Hanes 1974; Hall and Turner 1971).

Additionally, the past tense -ed and the negation *not* are included in sentence repetitions equally as frequently by Black and White children. Only the possessive 's and the plural third person -s tend to be unique omissions of Black children (Hall and Turner 1974). When both Black and White children read, the tendency is toward less use of standard English (Hall and Turner 1972); that is, both evidence omission.

The above studies raise serious questions for perceiving Black children's omissions in speech (imitation and reading) as a language deficiency. It has been suggested by some investigators of language that the deficits identified resulted from the setting in which language was sampled (Cazden 1970; Labov 1970). These settings were not seen as conducive to expressive language. Another interpretation offered by Anastasiow and Hanes (1974) is that language omissions reflect the children's level of cognitive development. They found that some Piagetian tasks (discrimination, seriation, and numeration) predicted the language performance of

Black and Anglo kindergarten and first and second graders equally as well; children at the same cognitive level, whether inner-city Black or middle SES White, performed equivalently on the imitation of sentences.

LANGUAGE AND THE DIFFERENT HYPOTHESIS

The deficit view, with its source of language deficiency within Black children resulting from experience, has been questioned by a number of writers (Baratz 1970; Cohen and Cooper 1972; Houston 1970; Labov 1970) who perceive language within a sociolinguistic frame of reference. They suggest that Black children's language is a fully developed vernacular; it simply differs in some aspects from standard English (SE) but is not inferior. Several studies support this position (Marwit and Marwit 1973; Marwit, Marwit, and Boswell 1972; Osser, Wang, and Zaid 1969) which is typically identified as the "different" hypothesis. It asserts that Black children's language should be treated like any other language system (French, Spanish, etc.). Compensatory educational practices derived from this hypothesis include: (1) teachers who understand the Black vernacular, accept and utilize it for encouraging school achievement and/or (2) teaching SE as a second language. Both of the foregoing practices have been used as means for enhancing Black children's success in school (Somervill 1975).

Although the different language view seems to require more respect for the psychoemotional-self of the child and for his or her culture, implicit in this position is that the different language creates difficulty in school due to its mismatch with the school language (Baratz 1969; Cazden 1970). Black children's different language still leaves them at a disadvantage in school tasks, presumably because the difference affects comprehension of SE.

In addition to the language reconstruction data (Anastasiow and Hanes 1974), other evidence is contrary to this prediction. Comprehension has been found to be independent of language type, i.e., SE and Black English (BE) for low SES Black children, when measured by pictures depicting the meaning of sentences (Hall and Turner 1971, 1972; Hall, Turner, and Russell 1973), word lists varying in syntactical structure (Weener 1969), the Stanford-Binet (Quay 1971, 1972), and standardized reading passages (Marwit and Newman 1974; Nolen 1972). However, in at least two studies, reading comprehension improvement was found to favor BE (Potter 1968; Somervill and Jacobs 1972). Each of these investigations included child-created stories. Perhaps it was not language type but interest-attraction that influenced the comprehension.

Perhaps treating BE as the primary language may be beneficial; it is not at all certain that the benefits relate to cognitive performance. The assumptions of the different language view have not received outstanding support. From the evidence to date, there is little reason to believe that BE yields better comprehension than SE. Certainly for receptivity of oral SE, Black children manifest little or no comprehension difficulties (Hall and Turner 1971; Peisach 1965; Somervill and Jacobs 1972). The conclusion by Hall and Turner (1974) seems quite valid: "In general, no acceptable, replicated research has found that the dialect spoken by black children presents them with unique problems in comprehending SE. If there are problems, they occur in relatively rare cases" (p. 79).

LANGUAGE AND MEMORY

Children's language knowledge has to be retained so that it is usable at appropriate times. To retain language, children code it in some form in their memory. These memorial codes become a basis for converting new to-be-remembered (TBR) information into meaningful codes for storage. Memory storage is generally thought to be verbal and imaginal. Verbal storage may be conceptualized as a system of semantic information. To use the example of the child playing with a dog, as the child learns the attributes of a dog, they become a part of his or her memorial semantic information of *dog*. When learning a new attribute such as "a dog has fangs," the child may use *dog* to incorporate *fang* into memory. In a sense the child tags *fang* by *dog*.

Remembering requires children to perceptually analyze the physical attributes of the TBR information. That is, children have to recognize the TBR event by attending to shape, phonology, position, temporal spacing, etc. (Craik and Lockhart 1972). Then they encode the TBR event in some manner that makes it meaningful to them and that increases ease of access at some later time. When the TBR event is verbal, children apply their preexisting semantic information (Murdock 1974; Tulving 1972) to some degree for retaining the event. Children store the representation along with its mnemonic tags. The memory tags may be associative and conceptual verbal terms, item groups or chunks, sequence or setting markers, selected components of the total event, or hierarchical organizers (Ausubel 1963; Bower 1972). Accomplishment of this acquisition, storage, and retrieval of information seemingly entails to some degree many of the cognitive functions in which Black children have been characterized as deficient (Gordon 1970). The statement by Hagen and his coworkers (Hagen, Jongeward, and Kail 1975) that knowledge of memorial processes may "provide some critical insights for our understanding of cognitive processes at a more general level" (p. 58) suggests the appropriateness of an examination of memory for understanding Black children's cognitive capabilities. A central issue is whether the Black child remembers by rote or by conceptualization (Jensen and Frederiksen, 1973).

MEMORIAL ACQUISITION

Beginning around age five or six, it seems that conceptual processing is more beneficial to the child than rote processing during acquisition.

Acquisition in memory refers to the intake of TBR information including such processes as attention, recognition, and encoding. There are numerous mnemonic encoding techniques. Among the conceptual encoding techniques are thinking of rhymes, category labels, and common associates; rote encoding techniques include repetition and remembering position.

One factor influencing encoding of the TBR event during acquisition is the structure of the information. A word list that is to-be-remembered may contain words that can be classified by category as shown in the right-hand columns of Table 1 or words that are unrelated as in the left-hand columns of Table 1. It is assumed that different list structures provoke different encoding techniques. A categorizable list is held to require conceptual processing since the most appropriate procedure is use of the categories. On the other hand, an unrelated word list is seen as requiring rote processing since it is difficult to form any within list groupings.

Table 1. Free Recall Word Lists

Unrelated word list		Categorized list	
sun	girl	horse	dog
wheel	bag	coat	bread
fish	tree	egg	dress
ball	road	bed	clock
pen	heart	skirt	apple
ship	money	lamp	sheep
salt	bee	cow	table
nest	cup	shoe	corn
box	eye	milk	hat
door	cake	chair	cat

If Black children have to rely on rote ability because they have limited conceptual skills as has been claimed (Jensen and Frederiksen 1973), then list structure would not affect their recall. Black children would deploy "brute force" regardless of what had to be remembered and would remember about the same amount for all types of information. Usually children recall a categorized list better than an uncategorized list (Jablonski 1974). This would be expected since conceptual processing, which begins to dominate mental activity around age six, yields more information. The evidence shows that Black children perform similarly; they earn higher scores on categorized lists (Grimmett 1975a; 1975b; Mensing and Traxler 1973).

Theoretically, conceptual processing of a categorized list should interfere with intake of an unrelated word list that follows immediately. Encoding by categorized concepts is difficult to apply in situations where each word belongs to a different category or where relationships among words are rather obscure. On the other hand, rote processing of unrelated words may be used for acquiring a categorizable list. Under such circumstances, both lists would be recalled about equally as well. This pattern of no difference in recall when a categorized list immediately follows an uncategorized list and higher recall of a categorized list when it precedes an uncategorized list would suggest the ability to conceptually process information. Figure 1 shows such a pattern obtained for Black

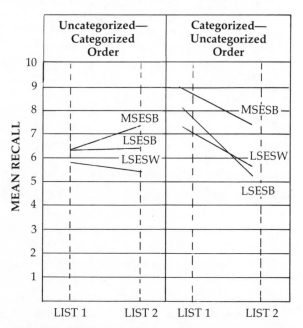

Figure 1. Order by list interaction of recall for each race-socioeconomic-status group.

and Anglo children (Grimmett 1975b). It can be speculated from Figure 1 that both ethnic groups used rote processing in the uncategorized-categorized list order and conceptual processing in the categorized-uncategorized list order. It seems that the kinds of processing children use depend upon immediate prior experience.

In addition to the effect of list structure on processing during acquisition is learning to take advantage of the structure of the information. A child may not know the most effective encoding technique. When taught, the child becomes able to use that encoding process. However, instructional benefits, in this instance, depend upon the child's having the necessary cognitive mechanisms. Without the requisite mechanisms, only massive instruction over an extended period would yield, if then, improvement in encoding. On the other hand, a child may have available appropriate techniques but not recognize their utility for a given task. Instruction would assist the child in identifying and matching encoding technique with TBR event. Being taught, in this instance, helps the child to develop a plan for remembering that is a "good fit" to the task.

Several studies have shown that short-term teaching of conceptual encoding techniques increases children's recall (Moely, Olson, Halwes and Flavell 1969; Shultz, Charness, and Berman 1973). Similar short-term instruction has improved the recall of young Black children (Grimmett 1975a). When older Black children have been asked how they go about remembering in the absence of instruction, they report a rote process (Table 2, Standard Group). Short-term instruction on how to elaborate cognitively TBR information by organizing it into categories and counting the items belonging to each category has improved recall (Minor 1974). Black children given such instruction report using this encoding technique (Table 2, Elaboration).

The recall of the TBR list by those children who reported using rote encoding after being instructed in such a process was no better than those children who spontaneously used similar

Table 2. Types of Reported Mnemonic Strategies of the Three Training Groups

Explanation	Elaboration	Training Repetition	Standard
Categories	22	3	2
Repetition (Memorized)	3	22	23
Other	1	1	3
No Response	4	4	4

(From Minor 1974)

rote procedures (Table 2). Whether instruction in conceptual memorial techniques facilitated remembering by providing a new encoding technique or by influencing the memorial planning of the Black child is unclear. What is evident is that Black children have the requisite cognitive mechanisms for conceptual memorial processing. Additionally, it is apparent that instruction tapping into Black children's spontaneous means of remembering does not necessarily assist these children in taking advantage of the structure of the information during acquisition. This impact of instruction on Black children's memorial performance indirectly indicates the devastating effects of assuming that Black children acquire TBR information by rote and that instruction should be based on enhancing the *nonconceptual* skills of Black children.

MEMORIAL STORAGE AND RETRIEVAL

The mental manipulation of TBR information during acquisition influences storage and retrieval. Conceptual encoding presumably requires utilization of children's pre-existing semantic networks, permitting storage according to meaningful relationships. Retrieval is the decoding of these relationships which may be reflected at the time of output. Clustering is a retrieval index that reflects how information was reorganized in storage and is a rather direct indicant of conceptual organization of information. Categorical clustering is a measure of se-

quential recall of items belonging to the same category. Since storage and retrieval are related to acquisition, clustering would be affected by prior experience. Figure 2 shows that prior experience has similar influence on Black and Anglo children. When the children recall an uncategorized list before a categorized list (experimental group), clustering decreases in comparison to recall of a categorized list only (control group; Grimmett 1976). It can be seen in Figure 2 that Black children benefited more than Anglo children when not having the prior different kind of list. They outdistanced the Anglo group by about eight percentage points for the amount of clustering.

Categorical clustering increases when the child is presented TBR information organized by category (Cole, Frankel, and Sharp 1971), a finding also obtained on Black children. When Black children are permitted to use their own notions as the basis for organizing information, clustering is greatly improved. This suggests that Black

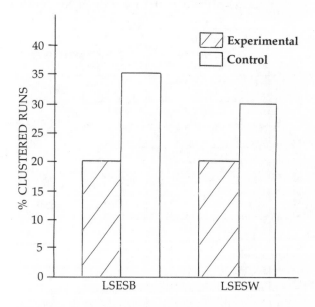

Figure 2. Percent of runs where two or more words from the same category were recalled by experimental and control groups of each race-socioeconomic-status group.

children are actively storing information in an organized fashion but the organization may differ from that of adults. Typically children form more categories with fewer items per category when asked to sort than do adults, an indication that children's meaning systems differ from adults' meaning systems. Although Black children's semantic systems may differ from the systems of adults they use them to advantage in storing and retrieving information.

Some of the meanings and concepts used for storage by children are similar to those used by adults, as attested to in the study of retrieval cues. For a retrieval cue to be effective, presumably the TBR information was tagged by that cue during acquisition, otherwise it would not be useful for decoding. It has been found in unreported research by the author that Black fourth grade children, though not first grade children, given category retrieval cues, recall more information than when not given such cues. Apparently Black children used the category labels to tag the incoming information. This finding also indicates that Black children acquire more information than is reflected in performance, as has been found for other children when presented retrieval cues (Halperin 1974; Kobasigawa 1974; Scribner and Cole 1972). The ineffectiveness of category cues for the Black first grade children studied may mean that they encoded by a different way or they encoded by categorical concepts but included so few words within the category that the cue was of no assistance. It has been reported that young children's recall may be unaffected by retrieval cues (Lange 1973).

MEMORY AND THE DIFFERENT HYPOTHESIS

From the evidence, there is no indication that Black children remember by a means that differs from Anglo children. The patterns of remembering shown in Figures 1 and 2 reveal that influences on memory have the same effect for Black and Anglo children. Similarity of memory pattern is a rather powerful invalidation of the different hypothesis which would require performance pattern differences. For example, if clustering had been higher for Black children after recall of uncategorized lists, and lower when recalling only a categorized list, with the reverse obtained for Anglo children, then there would be a different pattern for Black children suggestive of a different way for remembering. In the results reviewed here no such pattern differences were found. When pattern differences between Black and Anglo children have been found, the cognitive behavior was measured by standardized tests (Jensen 1974; Lesser, Fifer, and Clark 1965). Using such results, as well as findings from his memory studies, Jensen (1969) concluded that Black children are deficient in conceptual processing abilities. He stipulated that Black children learn by rote and Anglo children learn by conceptualization.

One difference between standardized test and memory test situations is that the former assesses learning less directly than the latter. In direct learning contexts, the commonality of experience does not have to be assumed whereas common learning experiences are assumed on standardized measures. If Black and Anglo children have not had common experiences, then the pattern differences found for standardized tests are difficult to claim as indexes of different ways of learning. By implication, standardized measures indicate the need for assuring that the learning context is equally powerful for all children. In the situations reported here, Black children were given individual attention as were Anglo children. Consequently many of the factors such as attending to the task, understanding the instructions, and the "catch-all" rapport that creates experiential differences were equalized. Under such circumstances Black children were not different from other children or deficient in remembering.

It could be claimed, however, that differences in ways of remembering between Black and Anglo children would be detected on examination of sensory modalities. Black children have been characterized as preferring to learn through their motor system or by nonverbal means (Reissman 1962). While there have been very few studies assessing sensory modality effects on memory for children belonging to different ethnic groups, the evidence that does exist indicates that Black and Anglo children are quite similar for the influence of sensory modality on memory (Williams, Williams, and Blumberg 1973).

Whether Black children remember differently or as much as Anglo children seems to depend on the nature of the task (Jensen et al. 1973; Semler and Iscoe 1963) and confounding of race and socioeconomic status (Rohwer, Ammon, Suzuki, and Levin 1971). Amount of performance at any given time relies so heavily upon the situational context—e.g., comfort of the child, understanding task requirements, task stimuli, etc., in addition to the overlay of beliefs held by the child and the investigator— that to equate amount of performance as synonymous with learning competency is hazardous (Ginsburg 1972). As any beginning psychology student knows, it is fallacious to view learning and performance as the same phenomenon. From the evidence here, there is no valid claim that inner-city Black children are incompetent or deficient in memorial processing. To the degree that memory includes perception and conception, then the data indicate that these processes are available to and used by Black children. Low SES Black children are no more rote memorizers than their Anglo counterparts.

INFORMATION PROCESSING COMPETENCE

The findings reviewed in this paper on language and memory as indexes of basic cognitive functions indicate that the mental processes upon which education is based are neither deficit nor different for inner-city children. However, the notion that inner-city Black children are poorly equipped and/or differently equipped for learning in schools still persists (Langer 1972). This perspective tends to blind us to the quality of behavior shown by Black children. Instead of viewing these children's learning performance as reflecting comprehension of language and other symbolic events, the performance is viewed as inadequate, dysfunctional, or interfering in the very cognitive processes under examination. Preconception of the behavior implies imperception of the behavioral reality. In effect, this perspective derived from assumptions of deficit and different leads to stereotypic judgments that disvalue Black children's cognitive skills (Crowl and MacGinitie 1974).

If assumptions could be set aside, these data on language and memory describe inner-city Black children as engaging in valuable mental manipulation of the information they are experiencing. In language they discriminate the verbal event from all events, reorganize it as reflected in paraphrasing, and comprehend it as indicated by such activities as answering questions and selecting pictures. To remember, Black children discriminate the TBR event from all other possible events, store it in semantically meaningful ways, reorganize it as reflected by clustering and reconstruction, and recall the TBR event. There is no question that the children can evidence these basic skills; the question is the expectations we as educators and researchers have for the evidentiary behavior.

RECOMMENDED RECONCEPTUALIZATION

To reexamine our expectations for inner-city Black children's cognitive performance we need to ask: How valid are our descriptions of cognitive function? How inclusive are our descriptive classifiers? Are our descriptions developmentally related as opposed to racially circumscribed? Are we expecting deployment of cognitions that necessitate teaching for manifestation? Some hints related to these questions can be extrapolated from the empirical results.

Valid description of a cognitive skill requires its evaluation in many different situations using many different tasks (Shipman 1974; Smilansky 1974). A child may have a competence but the range of contexts in which the competence is displayed may be limited either because no one has helped the child integrate the competence and context or because the child fails to recognize the appropriateness of the competence to the context. The notion of memorial plans includes the possibility of a plan being at variance with the optimal skill. Limited evaluation negates the chance of determining whether the skill is unavailable or whether it is simply unavailable in that context.

The use of racial categories to classify simultaneously cognitive functioning leads to the perception that all inner-city Black children are alike. Yet, we know that they are not a homogeneous group. Inner-city Black children differ in SES membership, ability, attitudes about learning, motivation for learning, feelings of importance and belongingness, and beliefs about being in control of one's learning. While the reported studies did not address attitudes and values, other documentations (Shipman 1974) have shown that these values affect what the children learn and under what circumstances they manifest the learning. Perhaps race has been used as a classifier because it seems easier to define than some other personal dimension. However, these other dimensions may be far more meaningful as a basis for designing educational programs. The historic confounding in many research studies of race and SES when determining Black children's ability to learn makes suspect the use of race as a critical dimension for educational planning. We need to be aware of potential confoundings in our classificatory schemes. These confoundings may mitigate the accuracy and effectiveness of our knowledge.

Our past characterization of Black children often could be interpreted within a developmental or theoretical frame of reference. For example to say that the young Black school child is motoric could easily be viewed within Piaget's concrete operation stage which lasts until about age 12 or so and connotes acquisition through direct handling of information. Or the ascription to Black children of misinterpretation of if-then syntactical constructions could well have been

attributed to development and not race (Anastasiow and Hanes 1974). Additionally the memory results revealed similar memorial patterns for Black and White children and showed that Black children deploy information processing as predicted from theoretical statements. Such performance supports the notion that some frame of reference other than race is needed for describing these children's behavior.

Finally, one facet of instruction is to teach children how to know the world. The power of instruction to facilitate extension and expansion of basic cognitive skills was quite obvious in some of the memory studies. Instruction helped to optimize more effectively and efficiently knowing how to remember. Smilansky (1974) found that disadvantaged children "know how to know the world" best when given the opportunity to use a cognitive skill in many different activities (e.g., drawing, reading, clay, dramatic play). Importantly, the fewer the activities the more ineffective the knowing "how to know." If low SES Black children are to know how to know the world, we must teach for transfer of learning. Children should not be left entirely on their own to fit things together; instruction must be directed toward integrating abilities across tasks and within tasks. The commonality of discrimination, concept identification, and comprehension through restatement for language and memory suggest basic abilities that may be integrated with rather divergent tasks.

Obviously all of the data are not in on basic cognitive processing of inner-city Black children. The recent evidence obtained for language and memory performance indicates that these children are competent in knowing how to know the world. This is not a claim that some Black children may not have deficiencies in information processing. It is a claim that race as a designation of deficiencies is untenable. As additional information on basic cognitive processes accrues, perhaps careful consideration of the posed questions will permit conceptualization of educational programs for inner-city Black children that increases each child's control of knowing how to know the world. Hopefully, it cannot be said at the advent of the 1980s what was said at the beginning of this decade: "Compensatory education may be a fraud perpetrated upon a poor and unsuspecting citizenry which has traditionally looked to education to lead it out of bondage" (Winschel 1970, p. 3).

References

Anastasiow, N.J., and Hanes, M.L. "Cognitive Development and the Acquisition of Language in Three Subcultural Groups." *Developmental Psychology* 10 (1974): 703-709.

Ausubel, D. P. *The Psychology of Meaningful Verbal Learning.* New York: Grune & Stratton, 1963.

Baratz, J. C. "A Bidialectal Task for Determining Language Proficiency in Economically Disadvantaged Negro Children." *Child Development* 40 (1969): 889-902.

Baratz, J. C. "Teaching Reading in an Urban Negro School System." In *Language and Poverty,* edited by F. Williams, Chicago: Markham Publishing Co., 1970.

Bereiter, C., and Englemann, S. *Teaching Disadvantaged Children in the Preschool.* Englewood Cliffs, N.J.: Prentice-Hall, 1966.

Bever, T. G. "The Cognitive Bases for Linguistic Structure." In *Cognition and the Development of Language,* edited by J. R. Hayes. New York: John Wiley & Sons, 1970.

Blank, M., and Solomon, T. "How Shall the Disadvantaged Child Be Taught?" *Child Development* 40 (1969): 47-61.

Bloom, B. S.; Davis, A.; and Hess, R. D. *Compensatory Education for Cultural Deprivation.* New York: Holt, Rinehart and Winston, 1965.

Bower, G. H. "Stimulus-Sampling Theory of Encoding Variability." In *Coding Processes in Human Memory,* edited by A. W. Melton and E. Martin. New York: John Wiley & Sons, 1972.

Bruner, J. S.; Oliver, R. R.; and Greenfield, P. M. *Studies in Cognitive Growth.* New York: John Wiley & Sons, 1966.

Cazden, C. "The Situation: A Neglected Source of Social Class Differences in Language Use." *Journal of Social Classes* 26 (1970): 35-60.

Cole, M.; Frankel, F.; and Sharp, D. "Free Recall Learning in Children." *Developmental Psychology* 4 (1971): 109-123.

Cohen, S. A., and Cooper, T. "Seven Fallacies: Reading Retardation and the Urban Disadvantaged Beginning Reader." *Reading Teacher* 26 (1972): 38-45.

Craik, F. I., and Lockhart, R. S. "Levels of Processing: A Framework for Memory Research." *Journal of Verbal Learning and Verbal Behavior* 11 (1972): 671-684.

Crowl, T. K., and MacGinitie, W. H. "The Influence of Students' Speech Characteristics on Teachers' Evaluations of Oral Answers." *Journal of Educational Psychology* 66 (1974): 304-308.

Deutsch, C. "Education for Disadvantaged Groups." *Review of Educational Research* 35 (1965): 140-146.

Deutsch, M. "The Role of Social Class in Language Development and Cognition." *American Journal of Orthopsychiatry* 35 (1965): 78-88.

Ervin-Tripp, S. "Some Strategies for the First Two Years." In *Cognitive Development and the Acquisition of Language,* edited by T. E. Moore. New York: Academic Press, 1973.

Ginsburg, H. *The Myth of the Deprived Child: Poor Children's Intellect and Education.* Englewood Cliffs, N.J.: Prentice-Hall, 1972.

Gordon, E. W. "Problems in the Determination of Educability in Populations with Differential Characteristics." In *Disadvantaged Child,* vol. 3, edited by J. Hellmuth. New York: Brunner/Mazel, 1970.

Grimmett, S. A. "A Pilot Study of the Effects of Prior Free Recall on Secondary Organization of Fourth Graders." *Journal Supplement Abstract Service, Catalog of Selected Documents in Psychology* 6 (1976): 9.

Grimmett, S. A. "Black and White Children's Free Recall of Unorganized and Organized Lists: Jensen's Level I and Level II." *Journal of Negro Education* 44 (1975a): 24-33.

Grimmett, S. A. "Free Recall of Categorized and Uncategorized Lists by Black and White Fourth Graders: A Test of Jensen's Theory." Institute for Child Study, Indiana University, 1975b.

Hagen, J. W.; Jongeward, R. H., Jr.; and Kail, J. R. V. "Cognitive Perspectives on the Development of Memory." In *Advances in Child Development and Behavior,* vol. 10, edited by H. W. Reese. New York: Academic Press, 1975.

Hall, V. C., and Turner, R. R. "Comparisons of Imitation and Comprehension Scores Between Two Lower-Class Groups and the Effects of Two Warm-Up Conditions on Imitation of the Same

Groups." *Child Development* 42 (1971): 1735-1750.

Hall, V. C., and Turner, R. R. *The Influence of Speaking Negro Nonstandard English on the Abilities to Imitate and Comprehend Standard English: Review and Recommendation.* Final Report submitted to National Program in Early Childhood Education, 1972.

Hall, V. C., and Turner, R. R. "The Validity of the 'Different Language Explanation' for Poor Scholastic Performance by Black Students." *Review of Educational Research* 44 (1974): 69-81.

Hall, V. C.; Turner, R. R.; and Russell, W. "The Ability of Children from Four Subcultures and Two Grade Levels to Imitate and Comprehend Crucial Aspects of Standard English: A Test of the Different Language Explanations." *Journal of Educational Psychology* 64 (1973): 147-158.

Halperin, M. S. "Developmental Changes in the Recall and Recognition of Categorized Word Lists." *Child Development* 45 (1974): 144-151.

Houston, S. H. "A Reexamination of Some Assumptions about the Language of the Disadvantaged Child." *Child Development* 41 (1970): 947-963.

Jablonski, E. M. "Free Recall in Children." *Psychological Bulletin* 81 (1974): 522-539.

Jensen, A. R. "How Much Can We Boost I.Q. and Scholastic Achievement?" *Harvard Educational Review* 39 (1969): 1-123.

Jensen, A. R. "Interaction of Level I and Level II Abilities with Race and Socioeconomic Status." *Journal of Educational Psychology* 66 (1974): 99-111.

Jensen, A. R., and Frederiksen, J. "Free Recall of Categorized and Uncategorized Lists: A Test of the Jensen Hypothesis." *Journal of Educational Psychology* 65 (1973): 304-312.

John, V. P., and Goldstein, L. S. "The Social Context of Language Acquisition." *Merrill-Palmer Quarterly of Behavior and Development* 10 (1964): 265-275.

Kobasigawa, A. "Utilization of Retrieval Cues by Children in Recall." *Child Development* 45 (1974): 127-134.

Labov, W. "The Logic of Nonstandard English." In *Language and Poverty,* edited by F. Williams. Chicago: Markham Publishing Co., 1970.

Lange, G. "The Development of Conceptual and Rote Recall Skills among School Age Children." *Journal of Experimental Child Psychology* 15 (1973): 394-406.

Langer, J. H. "The Disadvantaged, the Three R's, and Individual Differences." In *Education and the Many Faces of the Disadvantaged,* edited by W. W.

Brickman and S. L. Lehrer. New York: John Wiley & Sons, 1972.

Lesser, G.; Fifer, F.; and Clark, D. H. "Mental Abilities of Children from Different Social Classes and Cultural Groups." *Monograph of the Society for Research in Child Development* 30, no. 4 (1965): 102.

Marwit, S. J., and Marwit, K. L. "Grammatical Responses of Negro and Caucasian Second Graders as a Function of Standard and Nonstandard English Presentation." *Journal of Educational Psychology* 65 (1973): 187-191.

Marwit, S. J.; Marwit, K. L.; and Boswell, J. J. "Negro Children's Use of Nonstandard Grammar." *Journal of Educational Psychology* 63 (1972): 218-224.

Marwit, S. J., and Newman, G. "Black and White Children's Comprehension of Standard and Nonstandard English Passages." *Journal of Educational Psychology* 66 (1974): 329-332.

McNeill, D. *The Acquisition of Language: The Study of Developmental Psycholinguistics.* New York: Harper & Row, 1970.

Mensing, P. M., and Traxler, A. J. "Social Class Differences in Free Recall of Categorized and Uncategorized Lists in Black Children." *Journal of Educational Psychology* 65 (1973): 378-382.

Minor, B. J. "The Effects of Two Types of Training on Transfer Learning of High and Low Digit Span Black Children." Ph.D. dissertation, Indiana University, 1974.

Moely, B. E.; Olson, I. A.; Halwes, T. G.; and Flavell, J. H. "Production Deficiency in Younger Children's Clustered Recall." *Developmental Psychology* 1 (1969): 26-34.

Morehead, D. M., and Morehead, A. "From Signal to Sign: A Piagetian View of Thought and Language During the First Two Years." In *Language Perspective Acquisition, Retardation, and Intervention,* edited by R. L. Schiefelbusch and L. L. Lloyd. Baltimore: University Park Press, 1974.

Murdock, B. B. *Human Memory: Theory and Data.* New York: Halsted Press, 1974.

Nolen, P. S. "Reading Nonstandard Dialect Materials: A Study of Grades Two and Four." *Child Development* 43 (1972): 1092-1097.

Osser, H.; Wang, M. D.; and Zaid, F. "The Young Child's Ability to Imitate and Comprehend Speech: A Comparison of Two Subcultural Groups." *Child Development* 40 (1969): 1063-1075.

Passow, A. H., ed. *Education in Depressed Areas.* New

York: Teachers College, Columbia University, 1963.

Peisach, E. C. "Children's Comprehension of Teacher and Peer Speech." *Child Development* 36 (1965): 467-480.

Potter, T. C. "Reading Comprehension among Minority Groups: Child-Generated Instructional Materials." ERIC, ED 031 546, 1968.

Quay, L. C. "Language Dialect, Reinforcement, and the Intelligence-Test Performance of Negro Children." *Child Development* 42 (1971): 5-15.

Quay, L. C. "Negro Dialect and Binet Performance in Severely Disadvantaged Black Four-Year-Olds." *Child Development* 43 (1972): 245-250.

Reissman, F. *The Culturally Deprived Child.* New York: Harper & Row, 1962.

Rohwer, W. D., Jr.; Ammon, M. S.; Suzuki, N.; and Leven, J. R. "Population Differences and Learning Proficiency." *Journal of Educational Psychology* 62 (1971): 1-14.

Scribner, S., and Cole, M. "Effects of Constrained Recall Training on Children's Performance in a Verbal Memory Task." *Child Development* 43 (1972): 845-857.

Semler, I. J., and Iscoe, I. "Comparative and Developmental Study of the Learning Abilities of Negro and White Children under Four Conditions." *Journal of Educational Psychology* 54 (1963): 38-44.

Shipman, V. "Research Findings as Related to Educational Programming." Paper presented at the Indiana International Interdisciplinary Conference on Young Children, Indiana University, 1974.

Shultz, T. R.; Charness, M.; and Berman, S. "Effects of Age, Social Class, and Suggestion to Cluster on Free Recall." *Developmental Psychology* 8 (1973): 57-61.

Smilansky, S. "Some Main Dimensions of Educational Programming for Disadvantaged Young Children." Paper presented at the Indiana International Interdisciplinary Conference on Young Children, Indiana University, 1974.

Somervill, M. A. "Dialect and Reading: A Review of Alternative Solutions." *Review of Educational Research* 45 (1975): 256-262.

Somervill, M. A., and Jacobs, J. F. "The Use of Dialect in Reading Materials for Black Inner City Children." *Negro Educational Review* 23 (1972): 13-23.

Tulving, E. "Episodic and Semantic Memory." In *Organization in Memory,* edited by E. Tulving and W. Donaldson. New York: Academic Press, 1972.

Weener, P. D. "Social Class Dialect Differences and the Recall of Verbal Messages." *Journal of Educational Psychology* 60 (1969): 194-199.

Williams J.; Williams, D. V.; and Blumberg, E. L. "Visual and Aural Learning in Urban Children." *Journal of Educational Psychology* 64 (1973): 353-359.

Winschel, J. F. "In the Dark . . . Reflections on Compensatory Education, 1960-1970." In *Disadvantaged Child,* vol. 3, edited by J. Hellmuth. New York: Brunner/Mazel, 1970.

Valora Washington

Learning Racial Identity

Investigating the causes and effects of race awareness, racial attitudes, and racial identity is one of the most important sociopsychological tasks of American society. This problem has been unprecedented in its historic and continuing implications affecting most aspects of human relationships. There are several approaches to defining a race, which in turn reflect upon the varied interpretations of race awareness, racial attitudes, and racial identity. *Race* is generally defined as a social category based on biological characteristics, such as skin color, nasal index, and hair form (Porter 1971). Statutory/administrative conceptions upon which governmental actions are based include using one's ancestry or blood in establishing racial categories (Simpson and Yinger 1972). The "social" idea of race is that physical and behavioral traits are characteristically linked and that cultural achievements are determined by such linkages (Montagu 1971). Thus, race awareness is defined as knowledge of the visible biological differences between racial categories, which may serve as the perceptual clues used to classify people into particular social divisions.

Racial attitudes are also involved in this classification process. Krech and Crutchfield (1962) propose a definition which describes attitudes as a system including beliefs about objects, feelings toward them, and dispositions used to respond to them. Attitudes are learned, and there is a distinction between attitudes and their behavioral components, that is, the readiness with which they may be expressed in overt behaviors. Nonetheless, racial prejudice, a type of attitude based upon inflexible generalizations concerning specific racial/ethnic groups, involves a predisposition to respond to a certain stimulus in a predetermined manner (Porter 1971). Krech and Crutchfield acknowledge that persons organize the world around them through generalizations; however, ethnic organizations which include prejudicial racial attitudes add elements of rigidity, error, and hostility to these generalizations. Prejudices are thus attitudes holding affective or emotional quality that not all attitudes possess (Simpson and Yinger 1972).

This chapter will investigate factors involving how children, specifically Afro-American children, learn their racial identity as a consequence of their internalization of race awareness and racial attitudes.

HISTORICAL PERSPECTIVE

Not so very long ago, prominent scholars in various fields proposed that race awareness, racial attitudes, and racial identity were based on innate feelings. Thus, research in the area of racial identity was limited in the past due to the widely accepted belief of sociologists that racial attitudes were based upon consciousness of kind or inherent characteristics of the species specific to a particular race (Giddings 1896; Thomas 1904). The racial identity accompanying race awareness inevitably led people to discover that they were somehow superior or inferior, depending, of course, on the "kind" they were conscious about. According to early investigators, the racial attitudes acquired by children would appear to be expected and natural responses to their congenital status positions.

Indeed, these status positions were mandated by the peculiar history of race relations in the United States. Specifically, the very nature of the master-slave relationship persuasively indicated to many persons that the Western European was, at least originally, more advanced than the African genotypes in respect to their acquisition of skills necessary for human evolution in the modern world. Yet, speculation regarding the distribution of intelligence and mental capacities failed to justify the prespecification of human roles resulting from the legacy of the master-slave relationship. Thus, the laws organizing modern American life were forced to decree equality, regardless of race, creed, or national origin. Yet, these laws have been rendered inoperative in affecting social relationships. Although no chains continue to bind one human being to another, stereotypic racial categories remain traditional.

The perpetuation of relative inequalities between races raises the spectre of age-old questions regarding innate differences. Are there some biological determinants which cannot erase the relative advantage/disadvantage of groups approaching mutually accessible opportunities? Are there inherent prescriptions attached to race awareness and racial identity? Why is it that, over 100 years since the Emancipation Proclamation, Afro-American people have been hindered in their efforts to pull themselves up by their bootstraps by the Puritan work ethic which worked so well for the Pilgrims and White ethnic immigrants?

RESEARCH ON RACIAL IDENTITY

Only a few scholars would currently argue that race awareness, racial attitudes, and racial identity result from innate qualities and that abilities are racially determined. Many researchers assume an interactionist model, recognizing the influences of both nature and nurture in human development. Indeed, race awareness is described as a curiosity to children resulting from their increasing perceptual abilities. As children's perceptual acuity develops, so will their knowledge of racial differences, leading to differentiation between racial categories and the understanding of race as a social division as well as implications and expectations of their behavior as members of a particular racial group. The effect associated with racial differences reflects societal norms and values, not congenital superiority/inferiority. Thus, the notion of biological predisposition is not a valid explanation or rationale for racial prejudice and discrimination. Racial attitudes and racial identity are *learned*.

As a basis for examining the factors involved in this learning, one might first review the general findings upon which researchers have typically based their judgments about children's racial knowledge and racial identity. It is widely recognized that young children are aware of racial differences and that racial attitudes are formed during the earliest years of life (Ammons 1950; Landreth and Johnson 1953; Asher and Allen 1969).

Research has further indicated that racial recognitions occur by the third year of life and sharply increase in frequency with significant gains in the fourth year (Horowitz 1939; Clark 1939; Goodman 1946; Clark 1958; Morland 1958). However, in regard to their identities, Afro-American and White children are said to demonstrate differential performance in racial self-classification tasks. Goodman (1946) noted, as the Clarks (1958) later reaffirmed, that White children made more correct racial self-identifications than Afro-American children. The Afro-American children in Goodman's study, unlike the White children, were noted to display tension, uneasiness, and evasion when asked to make racial self-classifications. Although they were aware of racial differences, the Afro-American children were often unable to make correct self-identifications (Clark 1939, 1958).

Morland (1963) suggested that as White children became increasingly cognizant of racial differences, more of them tended to correctly classify themselves. However, increased racial awareness for Afro-American children decreased own-race identifications. When asked to state or select a preference, research indicates, according to the various instruments used in the studies, that Afro-American children preferred White skin, White dolls/puppets, and White friends, and that children of both races assigned poorer houses and less desirable roles to Black people (Clark 1939, 1958; Trager and Yarrow 1952). Thus, young children were aware of the social implications of race. In addition, there has been a noted tendency for Black children to assign negative roles to Afro-American children more frequently than White children assign such roles to children of their own race (Stevenson and Stewart 1958).

In accord with the pervasiveness of Anglo-Saxon cultural preference in the United States, many young children are thought to exhibit a cultural preference for White before they have a clear knowledge of how or why people are classified into racial groups. Consequent to these findings that Afro-American children are reluctant to acknowledge their Blackness, the research is thought to demonstrate the negative racial identity of these children. The racial identity learned by these children is said to cripple their emotional and cognitive development as a consequence of the negative connotations of Blackness and the emotional components accompanying racial prejudice.

These assertions, however, have not been unchallenged. For example, the 1966 study by Larson, Olson, Totdahl, and Jensen found that although Black children incorrectly identified themselves racially more often than White children, Afro-American children showed no significant preference for either race in their positive or negative role assignments to Black dolls and/or pictures.

Another significant departure from the negativism of earlier studies was demonstrated by Hodgkins and Stakenas (1969) on the effects of segregation and racial self-evaluations. Suggesting that a significant difference between Afro-Americans and Whites exists in self-adjustment and self-assurance in the school situation, with Blacks scoring slightly higher than Whites, self-perception was regarded as nondependent upon the values of the total society, but instead as dependent on people's judgments in terms of their total performance with regard to role expectations and significant others in their lives.

FACTORS INFLUENCING LEARNING

Despite the methodological problems and ideological controversy surrounding research on learning racial identity, researchers do not deny that the racial identity acquired by Afro-American children potentially affects their total development. Growing from interest in what children know and feel about racial differences, the factors influencing children's perceptions should be examined.

Whether Black children positively or negatively identify themselves as members of their race largely results from exposure to a variety of interrelated social influences, beginning with their earliest experiences (Clark 1955). Some of the influences are more direct than others, and the impact of specific phenomena may vary according to the age of the child, individual differences, and the socioeconomic status of the family. Research suggests that many of these factors (e.g., family, media, and/or schooling) foster, encourage, and/or reinforce stereotypic racial beliefs. Many studies concern the effects of a particular mechanism on existing attitudes at a particular period in the child's life. By isolating and combining possible influences in the child's environment shaping his or her racial identity, the interrelatedness and impact of these components can be stressed, examined, and assessed developmentally.

SIGNIFICANT OTHERS

Perhaps the most influential factor affecting the racial attitudes and racial identities which children learn is the relationships they develop with "significant others" in their lives. The earliest of these influences, initiated from within the family and training practices characterized by the home, largely contribute to the personality dimensions of racial identity. As children are desatellized from the home, the peer contacts and attitudes encountered may stimulate the social learning of racial concepts, affect perceptions of their racial identity, and provide instruction for race/culturally-related behavior. In addition, educators play a crucial role in the continued socialization of children (Foshay and Wann 1954). These significant others—parents, peers, and educators—have an accumulative impact upon developing children's responses to their own racial status.

Child Development and Childrearing Practices

The family is ascribed to be one of the most important agents of attitude transmission. Children accept parental norms through imitation and modeling behaviors, implicit and explicit teaching, overheard conversations, and subtle behavioral cues (Porter 1971). Yet, as is consistent with stimulus-response theory, the effects of reinforcement are often unnoticed as the source of reinforcement is often unrecognized by those who control it (Longstreth 1974).

However, one may logically assume that it is from these early experiences that children first become aware of themselves and are given first impressions of the world, including the importance of race relations in society. The adult's control of the child is evident in indications that infants by three months of age, and certainly by six months, are subject to social reinforcement. Furthermore, it has been demonstrated that the three-month-old children are differentially responsive to social reinforcers as presented by familiar and unfamiliar adult figures, as infants' discriminations of and attachments to specific individuals have significantly developed by this time (Wahler 1967).

Racial connotations may be presented to infants as soon as they are able to distinguish between familiar and unfamiliar persons. Children may reflect anxiety in contact with strangers, particularly if the stranger grabs the child, wears glasses, or has a different physical appearance such as skin color (Allport 1971). Nonetheless, instinctive fear of the strange, as it relates to the development of racial attitudes, need not be permanently and negatively fixated if a sense of security is developed as a result of children's personal/vicarious experiences or perceptions of their parents' reactions to racial differences (Harrison-Ross and Wyden 1973).

Reviews of intrafamily resemblances in personality characteristics also provide information that parents influence the development of attitudes, opinions, and interests of their children (Roff 1950). It has been proposed that, as topics beyond children's comprehension are directly/indirectly presented to them, they have no other alternative than to internalize parental values through patterns of identification (Porter 1971).

It has been indicated that socialization of children in the sense of control will not occur until the parents become reinforcers because socialization implies not only an object—the child—but also an agent—usually the parents (McCandless 1967). Thus, whether or not children develop ethnocentric attitudes may depend upon the methods of training used by the parents.

Accounts of prejudice and authoritarianism (Adorno, Fenkel-Brunswik, Levinson, Sanford 1950) conclude that parents of authoritarian, ethnocentric children use harsher, more rigid forms of discipline; insist on obedience; are more critical; more suppressive of children's impulses; more concerned with status and power than with love and affection; and do not use an individualized approach to the socialization of children; instead they are concerned with transmitting a set of fixed values and rules. Strict parents generally have more conflicts with children, and, as a consequence, children feel that parental love is conditional and therefore they have more experiences in which conforming behavior lessens anxiety. Consequently, children learn to mistrust their own impulses and, through projection, fear and are threatened by the impulses of others (Allport 1971).

It has been further hypothesized that ethnocentric children prescribe treatment for others which is comparable to that which they received from their parents (Radke 1946). Hence, children learn that power and authority dominate human relationships, and the concept of a hierarchal view of society is developed. In addition, Afro-American and/or low socioeconomic status families are thought to employ authoritarian punishment more often than middle socioeconomic status parents (Ausubel 1958; Ausubel and Sullivan 1970). High parental ethnocentrism associated with moderate punitiveness has also been found to be most conducive to childhood ethnocentrism (Epstein and Komorita 1966).

Other cultural and childrearing practices may further assist in the development of negative self-identity. Allport (1971) noted a nebulous sense of inferiority associated with dark skin due to its association with dirt. Harrison-Ross and Wyden (1973) add that some children confuse mud and feces with dark skin. From a psychoanalytic viewpoint, this negative racial connotation is thought to be a result of strict toilet-training practices. While children enjoy their bowel movements, the parents' negative reactions to them may negatively associate the color brown and feces with "bad" and "dirty." Thus, these toilet-training practices are thought to be more difficult for Afro-American children because the color of feces may closely resemble their skin color.

Allport makes a distinction between children's adoption of prejudice and the development of prejudicial attitudes. When children acquire attitudes from their family and environment through a transference of parental gestures, words, and beliefs, they are adopting prejudice. However, in another style of training, parents may or may not express their ideas to the child; rather, they create an atmosphere through which the child develops prejudice. In this style, the parental response to the child, the way the child is disciplined, loved, and threatened,

creates an atmosphere in which the child cannot help but develop suspicions, fears, and hatreds that will eventually become attached to minority out-groups. Allport suggests that these two modes of training usually interact.

Language development is also thought to have an impact on the development of racial connotations and the establishment of emotional responses which affect children's racial identity. The linguistic precedence in learning would imply that words having emotional or racist components are acquired and affect children before the referent to whom the words apply is known. However, when the referent is learned, children will already have developed racial connotations for the group.

Before Afro-American children are cognitively aware of their racial status, they may be affected by their parents' reactions to race. According to Ausubel and Sullivan (1970), the parents' reactions to their racial status may partly determine their acceptance/rejection of the child or their use of the child for their own ego-enhancement. It has been speculated that, in an environment of parental deprivations, tensions, resentment, and anger may surround children and make it impossible for them to develop a positive self-concept. Thus, Afro-American children affected in those ways may be more highly stimulated by race awareness and seek reassurance through activity and social contacts (Allport 1971).

Peer Interaction

Trager and Yarrow (1952) suggest that there is not a total correspondence between parental and child attitudes. Children are also influenced by their peers. Afro-American children in the inner city are free to join unsupervised play groups much earlier than the White suburban dweller. This is thought to be due to the more casual, less succorant caretaking considered to be characteristic of these families. Hence, the desatellization from parents which occurs during the middle childhood and preadolescence of middle socioeconomic status children is visible in low socioeconomic status children during the preschool and early elementary school years. During these years, the peer group assumes from the family the role of the prime socializing agent and source of value and derived status. Research has demonstrated that peer relationships do affect children's feelings about race (Horowitz 1947; Peck and Rosen 1965; Cantor 1973).

In this regard, the initiation of multicultural and varied socioeconomic status peer contacts is viewed as a significant beneift to be derived from desegregation schemes. However, interracial contact does not necessarily result in more positive attitudes (Horowitz 1947). Horowitz concluded that attitudes about Afro-Americans are not determined by contact with individuals but are primarily determined by contact with the prevalent attitudes in the culture.

Extending this argument, Black children may develop negative identity if, in the absence of intervention, they are exposed to societal low evaluations of Afro-Americans. Simpson and Yinger (1972) point out that racial prejudice can sometimes be explained as a result of interracial peer contacts, as the negative attitude represents a generalization of a few unpleasant experiences. This becomes a particularly crucial consideration in respect to the relationship between Black children's identity and recurrent conflicts which may involve some school busing schemes to achieve racial integration.

Teachers

Educators have been considered the most significant others in children's lives next to parents (Brookover and Erickson 1969). According to Davidson and Lang (1960), the assessment children make of themselves is related to the assessment which significant others make of them; specifically, children's self-appraisal may be related to the teacher's feelings. The more positive the child's perceptions of the teacher's feelings, the higher the child was rated by the teacher in terms of both academic achievement and classroom behavior. Teachers influence the racial identity of their students in both subtle

and overt ways. For example, by consciously/unconsciously accepting deprivation theories which state that low socioeconomic status Black children have irreversible cognitive deficits, such teachers will not be motivated to structure the learning environment which the children need. In addition, teachers believing in White superiority communicate that idea to children (Banks 1972).

Banks (1972) indicates that most White Americans have negative feelings toward Afro-Americans and suggests that teachers' attitudes are comparable to and reflect the majority position. Such negative attitudes are thought to result in the teachers' self-fulfilling prophecy of lower expectations for the Afro-American child.

The impact that low expectations have on student performance was discussed by Rosenthal and Jacobson (1968) who found that students who were expected to learn tend to achieve in school while those who were not expected to learn often become academic failures and dropouts. The effects of teacher expectations were most pronounced in the lower grades, where the children appeared to be most susceptible to the quality of teacher contact, e.g., facial expressions, tone of voice, and touch. Although this research has been criticized (Barber and Silver 1969a, 1969b), implications for possible influences on children's racial identities are evident and hence require further study.

Many teachers are either unaware of or insensitive to the types and nature of implicit and explicit teaching of negative racial attitudes within their classrooms. Color connotations through the use of value-laden words, and the denigration of the word *black* through its association with scary or undesirable phenomena, affect the child. As the implications of race as a social category are realized, Black people are associated with those negative color connotations in the larger society (Yancey and Singh 1973). Lack of teacher intervention in children's conversations concerning racial differences also plays a role in the transmission and maintenance of racial stereotypes.

It has also been suggested that the race of the teacher may influence the development of the Black child's identity. Gottlieb (1964) found that White teachers disliked teaching Black students more than Afro-American teachers did and that White teachers attributed more negative traits to the Black students. In discussing school problems, Afro-American teachers emphasized the need for improved physical facilities, while White teachers emphasized the children's "faults." Clark (1964) found that one-half of the White teachers studied felt that Afro-American students were innately inferior to White students and unable to learn in school.

Without processes to screen out or sensitize teachers holding these attitudes, their relationship to Black children, particularly elementary pupils, may be damaging. Considering these findings, it is not surprising to note that Afro-American students have been found to believe that their White teachers have low estimates of their ability and worth (Davidson and Lang 1960). Maehr and Rubovits (1973) compared the interactions of White female student teachers with students of comparable ability who were experimentally labeled as White gifted/nongifted and Black gifted/nongifted. The researchers found that Afro-American students were given less attention, ignored more, praised less, and criticized more often. In addition, the Black gifted child received the worst of that treatment, even in comparison to the Black non-gifted group.

OTHER CULTURAL TRANSMITTERS

As significant others affect the racial identities of children, they are also learning about race through environmental and cultural factors which transmit information and provide instruction. If these cultural models (e.g., media and school environment) neglect or negatively respond to the culture, history, language, and values of minority groups, messages containing unfavorable perceptions of one's racial/cultural status are realized.

Media

Media have been demonstrated to be a powerful and influential nonformal socialization agent. Visual stimuli greatly enhance the effectiveness of instructional attempts aimed at racial attitudes (Peterson and Thurstone 1933; Campbell and Stover 1933). The effects of media assume greater importance as one realizes that 93 percent of American homes have television sets (Sarson 1971). According to the Nielsen television index for preschool children age three to five who are at home, 64 percent of their waking hours, or 54 hours weekly, are spent watching television. In addition, low socioeconomic children tend to watch television more than children of higher socioeconomic status do (Liebert, Neale, and Davidson 1973). Race and ethnic differentials in viewing have not been substantiated for young children, although differences do exist for older children; that is, low socioeconomic status Blacks watch more than low socioeconomic status Whites.

Most of what children learn from television is considered incidental, as practically all of the child's use of media is for his or her entertainment. On the basis of the familiarity principle, children are more attentive to new facts and behaviors. Thus, the greatest amount of learning from television should occur between ages three and eight (Schramm, Lyle, and Parker 1961).

Nonetheless, "entertainment" of this nature communicates information to the child concerning the culture's social structure, and it shapes attitudes about one's self (Liebert, Neale, and Davidson 1973). Coles (1967) found that young children are interested in the race of television performers. Based on children's interest and attention to media, many investigators have lamented that television drama gives unproportional preference to White, middle socioeconomic status urban society; 80 percent of all characters were White (Smythe 1954) and minorities were more likely to be lawbreakers (Himmelweit, Oppenheim, Vince 1958; Brown 1969; Gerbner 1969, 1972). Gerbner notes that while television does not mirror the real world it does mirror its values. It has been suggested that television undergirds Black consciousness by limiting parts assigned to Afro-Americans to those acceptable to Whites, or by modernizing old stereotypes; the media message still emphasizes White cultural preferences and values (Arnez 1972; Simpson and Yinger 1972).

The media as represented through advertising and product packaging may also have negative implications for Black identity (Green 1975). Although some products exclusively marketed to Afro-Americans use Black models, the evaluative standards and norms generally expressed in advertising usually reflect Anglo preferences. It has been argued that demonstrating "Black is beautiful" concepts to children may be more difficult when they are exposed to virtually hundreds of messages each day which favor certain physical characteristics and values over others.

The Preschool and School Environment

Current practices within schools may also assist in the devaluation of the Black children's racial identity. In regard to these practices, the underlying values and middle socioeconomic status culture inherent in the school structure may do more harm than good in predominantly low socioeconomic status or culturally different schools (Ornstein 1968). Upward mobility among Blacks is thought to be inhibited because the schooling facilitating it alienates and isolates gifted students from their racial community and causes them to be ashamed of their culture and heritage. Ornstein suggests that ego-supporting and meaningful institutions which utilize rather than attempt to change the child's culture would be most beneficial for these children.

At present, desegregation of schools is the legally sanctioned method to eliminate inequalities in education. However, Armstrong and Gregor (1964) posit that Afro-American children's egos may be damaged if exposed to White rejection at an integrated school. Porter (1971) rejects that position by noting that the middle and working socioeconomic status children in desegregated settings more frequently classified themselves as Brown. However, Asher and Allen (1969) provide support for social comparison theory which predicts that desegregation will increase White preference among Afro-American children and compound their feelings of inferiority. Nonetheless, increased achievement among Afro-American students is regarded as a benefit to be derived from desegregation, particularly for those who enter integrated settings in the early grades. In terms of their ego development, Afro-Americans attending racially and economically heterogeneous schools are thought to compare themselves with actual models, therefore decreasing inferior self-judgments (Ausubel 1958).

Curriculum Content and Materials

Within the school structure, it is important that the total curriculum and approach to education emphasize and underline goals to enhance the individual's perceptions of self and others. In regard to racial attitudes, research indicates that teaching materials and methods can affect the racial feelings of students (Schoroff 1930; Remmers 1931; Johnson 1966; Litcher and Johnson 1969; Roth 1969; Yancey and Singh 1973). That research also demonstrated that specific efforts to enhance Black children's racial feelings through curriculum and teaching methods were successful.

Nonetheless, the materials often used to instruct Afro-American children do not provide opportunities to enhance their racial identities. In a comparative study of minorities in textbooks, the Committee on the Study of Teaching Materials in Intergroup Education (1949) found that Afro-Americans were frequently stereotyped in both elementary and high school texts. Marcus (1961) found few substantial changes from the 1949 study. Other reports (Stampp, Jordan, Levine, Middlekauff, Sellers, and Stocking 1964; Sloan 1966; Michigan State Department of Public Instruction 1968; Banks 1969; Kane 1970) have confirmed earlier findings.

GROUP DIFFERENCES

One's racial identity is also related to a range of individual differences which may be partly viewed in terms of one's unique mixture of certain measurable group differences, e.g., sex role and geographic location. That is, an individual's response to racial status may reflect that person's status as a White, low socioeconomic status southern female as contrasted to a northern, Afro-American, middle socioeconomic status, dark-complexioned male.

Sex Role

Due to the values defining, and the emphasis upon, female beauty, Black females have traditionally been considered most likely to be negatively affected by minority status in this respect. This is consistent with the finding that Black females have greater incidences of self-misidentification (Porter 1971) which may reflect wish-fulfillment.

In terms of their sex-role adjustments, however, Afro-American females are considered to have a favored position in comparison with White middle socioeconomic status females. Assuming the presence of the controversial matriarchal family atmosphere of Afro-American homes, this argument posits that these families sustain a preference for daughters, as opposed to the preference for sons in White, middle socioeconomic status patriarchal families (Ausubel 1958; Ausubel and Sullivan 1970). For this reason, Ausubel suggests that economically disadvantaged, segregated Afro-American females are less traumatized by racism than are their male counterparts. However, on the basis of racial self-classification, other research indicates that Afro-American females have a more negative, and White females a more positive, racial identity than their male counterparts (Porter 1971).

Geographic Location

Positive evaluations of Whites and negative evaluations of Afro-Americans have been documented in studies using both races in the North and South, and in segregated and integrated settings (Greenwald and Oppenheim 1968; Morland 1962; Goodman 1952; Stevenson and Stewart 1958). Of these groups, Afro-American children in the South have traditionally been considered most likely to reject their own race (Morland 1966). Regional differences have been noted in prejudice in the form of stereotyped belief about and behavior toward Afro-Americans, as race has historically been a more salient factor in sociocultural adjustment factors in the South (Pettigrew 1959).

Socioeconomic Status

Socioeconomic status may differentially affect children's acquisition of racial identity. Due to the earlier desatellization process considered characteristic of low socioeconomic status families (Ausubel 1958; Ausubel and Sullivan 1970), low socioeconomic status children may have earlier development of their racial identities as they are less protected from social realities.

Consistent with social comparison theory, which predicts increased White preference with increased social mobility, the middle socioeconomic status Afro-Americans in Porter's study (1971) made less frequent selections of the Black doll when asked to choose a preference. Spontaneous comments made by these children were indicative of own-race rejection in addition to White preference. However, comments made by the working class Blacks were more hostile toward Whites and showed more own-race acceptance and a more favorable self-concept. The reactions of the Black middle socioeconomic group are said to reflect their marginal status and feelings of dissatisfaction with own-race characteristics. The racial status of the middle socioeconomic groups may deny them the recognition usually accorded individuals on the basis of merit. Identification with the oppressive group and/or ambivalent or negative own-race identity are ways which some middle socioeconomic status Afro-Americans react to these conflicts. Porter also suggested the reactions of the working class children may result from the support provided for their racial status in the Black community.

SUPERIORITY RECONSIDERED: THE CULT OF CULTURAL DEPRIVATION

The literature on racial identity and the factors involved in its learning are characterized by serious methodological problems, including inadequate controls over salient factors such as skin color (for Blacks), socioeconomic status, and sex. Techniques have often been inappropriate. Children were often required to designate racial preferences by motor responses, such as pointing or choosing between alternatives. Their racial identities may be inferred from their choices by the investigator but may have an entirely different meaning for the children. The choice may represent a set response for the type of doll which children owned (the manufacture of Black dolls was not prevalent at the time of many studies). In addition, semantic difficulties involve the definitions of terms such as "White preference" and "Black rejection" and the ways in which these terms are used to interpret the children's functional responses. There is a possibility that children's responses were based upon their perceptions of the social and political realities they observed. The methodological problems of the research are partly responsible for the conflicting findings in the literature.

The literature on racial attitudes and racial identity is most consistent in its lack of a formal theoretical framework and theoretical orientation. However, a very pervasive informal orientation has been established as a framework for interpreting and assessing research results. The concept of cultural "deprivations" has been used to explain how factors involved in learning racial identity affect and cause the emotional and cognitive growth of Afro-American children.

Afro-American homes have been a primary suspect in contributing to children's incomplete identity. The literature seems to emphasize what is considered negative in the Black family. For example, Ausubel and Sullivan (1970) commented that the ego development of Black children may be dampened by their exposure to homes where there is parental deprivation, tension, anger, and resentment. Theories of identity propose that the economic position of Afro-Americans is important in developing their insecurity and restricting their initiative and societal trust (Erikson 1959).

Matriarchy, disorganization, and lack of intellectual values are other factors in the Black home which are cited as undesirable from the vantage point of White middle socioeconomic status culture. Yet, these contentions fail to acknowledge that the causes of "parental deprivations," societal distrust, racial oppression, and social inequities are institutionally perpetuated against Afro-Americans. The causes of those factors do not stem from within the Black culture.

In addition, these contentions fail to recognize that the "changeworthy" aspects of Afro-American culture may have profoundly different effects and serve different purposes for the group than they do for the White middle socioeconomic group. Ausubel and Sullivan point out that authoritarian childrearing practices are characteristic of Black homes. Yet, the effects of authoritarian practices were found to benefit the daughters of Black families, while causing personality maladjustments in White girls (Baumrind 1972).

It is suggested that social norms and historical factors influence the extent to which authoritarian childrearing practices are accompanied by the authoritarian personality syndrome, as characterized by Adorno, Fenkel-Brunswik, Levinson, and Sanford (1950). Thus Afro-American families may be characterized by the practices, but not the syndrome, e.g., dogmatic/intolerant attitudes. By evaluating Afro-American families by White middle socioeconomic status values, researchers disregard the effects of culturally determined norms on human development.

Furthermore, by emphasizing the presumed faults of Afro-American culture, attention is detracted from practices in the larger culture which impinge upon the Black community. With this approach, change is seen as desirable through a one-way process: from the Black cultural norms to desired structures as defined by a White middle socioeconomic status context. Thus, in order to achieve, it is the primary responsibility of the oppressed classes to end the cycle of the culturally-transmitted values inherent in their "heritage of slavery." Ryan (1971) argues that such explanations of the causes of poverty and negative self-esteem in Black communities allow for the perpetuation of racial stereotypes by substituting liberal, quasi-sociological rationales for crude racist ones.

The bias evident in these explanations is not dissimilar from the ideas presented by nineteenth century sociologists. In this regard, there are two schools of thought. In the first, scholars reviving the biological view maintain that racial attitudes and their social consequences can be up to 80 percent biologically determined. In the second "competing" view, it is argued that the social consequences of race are a product of environmental phenomena. Specifically, this view posits that Black children are handicapped by exposure to a deprived, deficit culture. However, with either explanation, the unit of analysis remains the inner-city racial enclave culture. With either school of thought, the victims of discrimination are seen as needing compensation for their "deprivations," and education and motivation to adapt to White middle socioeconomic status values. Both the biological and environmental arguments in this regard have models which emphasize the cognitive and affective weaknesses of inner-city Black children. These models appear to share premises deeply rooted in the ideology of racial/cultural supremacy or preference. Although the phraseology, intents, and social feelings between these schools may sometimes differ, each clearly communicates a hierarchy of culturally acceptable norms and values.

Thus, the pertinent interdisciplinary task facing those concerned about Afro-American children's racial identity is not only negating the deficit views extrapolated from the cultural factors involved in learning. Most importantly, examination of the factors involved in learning must assist efforts to identify, emphasize, and develop programs intended to capitalize upon the strengths of Black children who are presently or potentially negatively affected by social response to their race and culture.

References

Adorno, T.; Fenkel-Brunswik, E.; Levinson, D.; and Sanford, R. *The Authoritarian Personality*. New York: Harper & Row, 1950.

Allport, G. W. "Prejudice and the Young Child." In *Racism: A Casebook*, edited by F. R. Lapides and D. Burrows. New York: Thomas Y. Crowell Co., 1971.

Ammons, H. B. "Reactions in a Projective Doll Play Interview of White Males Two to Six Years Old to Differences in Skin Color and Facial Features." *Journal of Genetic Psychology* 76 (1950): 323-341.

Armstrong, C., and Gregor, A. "Integrated Schools and Negro Character Development." *Psychiatry* 27 (1964): 69-72.

Arnez, N. "Enhancing the Black Self-Concept Through Literature." In *Black Self-Concept*, edited by J. A. Banks and J. D. Grambs. New York: McGraw-Hill, 1972.

Asher, S. R., and Allen, V. L. "Racial Preferences and Social Comparison Processes." *Journal of Social Issues* 25 (1969): 157-166.

Ausubel, D. "Ego Development among Segregated Negro Children." *Mental Hygiene* 42 (1958): 362-369.

Ausubel, D., and Sullivan, E. *Theory and Problems of Child Development*. New York: Grune & Stratton, 1970.

Banks, J. A. "A Content Analysis of the Black American in Textbooks." *Social Education* 33 (December 1969): 954-957.

Banks, J. A. "Racial Prejudice and the Black Self-Concept." In *Black Self-Concept*, edited by J. A. Banks and J. D. Grambs. New York: McGraw-Hill, 1972.

Barber, T. X., and Silver, M. J. "Fact, Fiction, and the Experimenter Bias Effect." *Psychological Bulletin Monographs Supplement*, 1969-70a, pp. 1-29.

Barber, T. X., and Silver, M. J. "Pitfalls in Data Analysis and Interpretation: A Reply to Rosenthal."

Psychological Bulletin Monographs Supplement, 1969-70b, pp. 48-62.

Baumrind, D. "An Exploratory Study of Socialization Effects on Black Children: Some Black-White Comparisons." *Child Development* 43 (1972): 261-267.

Brookover, W. B., and Erickson, E. L. *Society, Schools and Learning.* Boston: Allyn and Bacon, 1969.

Brown, C. M. "What Lies Ahead for Black Americans?" *Negro Digest* 19 (November 1969): 34-36.

Campbell, D. W., and Stover, G. F. "Teaching International-Mindedness in the Social Studies." *Journal of Educational Sociology* 7 (1933): 244-248.

Cantor, G. N. "Effects of Familiarization on Children's Ratings of Pictures of Whites and Blacks." In *Child Development and Behavior,* edited by F. Rebelsky and L. Dorman. 2nd ed. New York: Alfred A. Knopf, 1973.

Clark, K. "Clash of Cultures in the Classroom." In *Learning Together,* edited by M. Weinberg. Chicago: Integrated Education Associates, 1964.

Clark, K. *Prejudice and Your Child.* Boston: Beacon Press, 1955.

Clark, K., and Clark, M. "The Development of Consciousness of Self and the Emergence of Racial Identity in Negro Preschool Children." *Journal of Social Psychology* 10 (1939): 591-599.

Clark, K., and Clark, M. "Racial Identification and Preference in Negro Children." In *Readings in Social Psychology,* edited by E. E. Maccoby et al. New York: Holt, Rinehart and Winston, 1958.

Coles, R. *Children of Crisis.* Boston: Little, Brown and Co., 1967.

Committee on the Study of Teaching Materials in Intergroup Education. *Intergroup Relations in Teaching Materials.* Washington, D.C.: American Council on Education, 1949.

Davidson, H., and Lang, G. "Children's Perceptions of Their Teachers' Feelings Toward Them Related to Self-Perception, School Achievement and Behavior." *Journal of Experimental Education* 29 (December 1960): 107-118.

Epstein, R., and Komorita, S. "Childhood Prejudice as a Function of Parental Ethnocentrism, Punitiveness, and Outgroup Characteristics." *Journal of Personality and Social Psychology* 3 (1966): 259-264.

Erikson, E. "Identity and the Life Cycle." *Psychological Issues* 15, Monograph 1 (1959).

Foshay, A., and Wann, K. *Children's Social Values.* New York: American Book-Stratford Press, 1954.

Gerbner, G. *The Film Hero: A Cross-Cultural Study.* Lexington, Ky.: Association for Education in Journalism, 1969.

Gerbner, G. "Violence in Television Drama: Trends and Symbolic Functions." In *Television and Social Behavior Vol. I: Media Content and Control,* edited by G. A. Comstock, E. A. Rubinstein, and J. Murray. Washington, D.C.: U.S. Government Printing Office, 1972.

Giddings, F. H. *Principles of Sociology.* New York: McMillan, 1896.

Goodman, M. E. "Evidence Concerning the Genesis of Interracial Attitudes." *American Anthropologist* 48 (1946): 624-630.

Goodman, M. E. *Race Awareness in Young Children.* Cambridge, Mass.: Addison-Wesley Press, 1952, 1964.

Gottlieb, D. "Teaching and Students; The Views of Negro and White Teachers." *Sociology and Education* 27 (Summer 1964): 345-353.

Green, C. "Manufactured White Racism." *Essence* 6 (May 1975): 8.

Greenwald, H., and Oppenheim, D. "Reported Magnitude of Self-Misidentification among Negro Children: Artifact?" *Journal of Personality and Social Psychology* 8 (1968): 49-52.

Harrison-Ross, P., and Wyden, B. *The Black Child—A Parent's Guide.* New York: Peter H. Wyden, 1973.

Himmelweit, H.; Oppenheim, A.; and Vince, P. *Television and the Child.* New York: Oxford University Press, 1958.

Hodgkins, B., and Stakenas, R. "A Study of the Self-Concepts of Negro and White Youth in Segregated Environments." *Journal of Negro Education* 38 (1969): 370-377.

Horowitz, E. "Development of Attitudes Towards Negroes." In *Readings in Social Psychology,* edited by E. E. Maccoby et al. New York: Holt, Rinehart and Winston, 1958.

Horowitz, R. "Racial Aspects of Self-Identification in Nursery School Children." *Journal of Psychology* 7 (1939): 91-99.

Johnson, D. "Freedom School Effectiveness: Changes in Attitudes of Negro Children." *Journal of Applied Behavioral Science* 2 (1966): 325-330.

Kane, M. *Minorities in Textbooks: A Study of Their Treatment in Social Science Texts.* Chicago: Quadrangle Books, 1970.

Krech, D., and Crutchfield, R. *Individual in Society.* New York: McGraw-Hill, 1962.

Landreth, C., and Johnson, B. "Young Children's Responses to a Picture and In-Set Test Designed to Reveal Reactions to Persons of Different Skin Colors." *Child Development* 24 (1953): 63-80.

Larson, R. G., et al. "Kindergarten Racism: A Projective Assessment." Unpublished report, University of Wisconsin, Milwaukee, 1966. (Arnez, N. "Enhancing the Black Self-Concept Through Literature." In *Black Self-Concept,* edited by J. A. Banks and J. D. Grambs. New York: McGraw-Hill, 1972.)

Liebert, R.; Neale J.; and Davidson, E. *The Early Window: Effects of Television on Children and Youth.* New York: Pergamon Press, 1973.

Litcher, J., and Johnson, D. "Changes in Attitudes Towards Negroes after Use of Multiethnic Readers." *Journal of Educational Psychology* 60 (1969): 248-252.

Longstreth, L. *Psychological Development of the Child.* New York: Alfred A. Knopf, 1974.

Maehr, M., and Rubovits, P. "Pygmalion Black and White." In *Child Development and Behavior,* edited by F. Rebelsky and L. Dorman. New York: Alfred A. Knopf, 1973.

Marcus, L. *The Treatment of Minorities in American History Textbooks.* New York: Anti-Defamation League, 1961.

McCandless, B. "The Socialization Process." In *The Child: A Book of Readings,* edited by J. M. Seidman, New York: Holt, Rinehart and Winston, 1969.

Michigan State Department of Public Instruction. *A Report on the Treatment of Minorities in American History Textbooks.* Lansing, Mich.: Michigan Department of Education, 1968.

Montagu, A. "Race: The History of an Idea." In *Race Awareness: The Nightmare and the Vision,* edited by R. Miller and P. J. Dolan. New York: Oxford University Press, 1971.

Morland, K. "Comparisons of Racial Awareness in Northern and Southern Children." *American Journal of Orthopsychiatry* 36 (1966): 22-32.

Morland, K. "Racial Acceptance and Preference of Nursery School Children in a Southern City." *Merrill-Palmer Quarterly* 8 (1962): 271-280.

Morland, K. "Racial Recognitions by Nursery School Children in Lynchburg, Virginia." *Social Forces* 37 (1958): 132-137.

Morland, K. "Racial Self-Identification: A Study of Nursery School Children." *American Catholic Sociological Review* 24 (1963): 231-242.

Ornstein, A. "Reaching the Disadvantaged." *School and Society* 96 (March 1968): 214-216.

Peck, S., and Rosen, S. "The Influence of the Peer Group on the Attitudes of Girls Towards Skin Color Differences." *Phylon,* Spring 1965, pp. 50-63.

Peterson, R., and Thurstone, L. *Motion Pictures and the Social Attitudes of Children.* New York: Macmillan, 1933.

Pettigrew, T. F. "Regional Differences in Anti-Negro Prejudice." *Journal of Abnormal and Social Psychology* 59 (1959): 28-36.

Porter, J. *Black Child, White Child: The Development of Racial Attitudes.* Cambridge, Mass.: Harvard University Press, 1971.

Radke, M. *Relation of Parental Authority to Children's Behavior and Attitudes.* Minneapolis, Minn.: University of Minnesota Institute of Child Welfare Monograph 22, 1946.

Remmers, H. H. "Propaganda in the Schools—Do the Effects Last?" *Public Opinion Quarterly* 2 (April 1931): 197-210.

Roff, M. "Intrafamily Resemblance in Personality Characteristics." *Journal of Psychology* 30 (1950): 199-227.

Rosenthal, R., and Jacobson, L. "Self-Fulfilling Prophecies in the Classroom; Teacher's Expectations as Unintended Determinants of Pupils' Intellectual Competence." In *Social Class, Race and Psychological Development,* edited by M. Deutsch, I. Katz, and A. Jensen. New York: Holt, Rinehart and Winston, 1968.

Roth, R. "The Effects of 'Black Studies' on Negro Fifth Grade Students." *Journal of Negro Education* 38 (Fall 1969): 435-439.

Ryan, W. *Blaming the Victim.* New York: Random House 1971.

Sarson E. *Action for Children's Television.* New York: Avon, 1971.

Schoroff, P. "An Experiment in the Measurement and Modification of Racial Attitudes of School Children." Ph.D. dissertation, New York University, 1930. (Banks, J. A. "Racial Prejudice and the Black Self-Concept." In *Black Self-Concept,* edited by J. A. Banks and J. D. Grambs. New York: McGraw-Hill, 1972.)

Schramm, W.; Lyle, J.; and Parker, E. *Television in the Lives of Our Children.* Stanford, Calif.: Stanford University Press, 1961.

Simpson, G., and Yinger, J. *Racial and Cultural Minorities: An Analysis of Prejudice and Discrimination.* New York: Harper & Row, 1972.

Sloan, I. *The Negro in Modern History Textbooks.* Chicago: American Federation of Teachers, AFL-CIO, 1966.

Smythe, D. "Reality as Presented by Television." *Public Opinion Quarterly* 18 (1954): 143-156.

Stampp, K.; Jordan, W.; Levine, L.; Middlekauff, R.; Sellers, C.; and Stocking, G. "The Negro in American History Textbooks." *Integrated Education* 2 (October-November 1964): 9-24.

Stevenson, H., and Stewart, E. "A Developmental Study of Racial Awareness in Young Children." *Child Development* 29 (1958): 399-409.

Thomas, W. I. "The Psychology of Race Prejudice." *American Journal of Sociology* 9 (March 1904): 593-611.

Trager, H., and Yarrow, M. *They Learn What They Live.* New York: Jaroer and Brothers, 1952.

Wahler, R. "Infant Social Attachments: A Reinforcement Theory, Interpretation, and Investigation." *Child Development* 38 (1967): 1079-1088.

Yancey, A., and Singh, J. "Black Is a Beautiful Color." *Today's Education* 62 (April 1973): 58.

Harvey A. Moore

Examining the Flat Ego: The Problem of Self-Concept, Race, and Social Myth

An important theme in the literature on minority education holds that inner-city children suffer from egos flattened[1] by the impact of race, culture, or socioeconomic status conflict (e.g., on Black self-concept, see Banks and Grambs, 1972; Fanon 1967; Kardiner and Ovessey 1952; or Grier and Cobbs 1968). Characteristic of this perspective is Grambs's observation, "The Negro experience *cannot* be unmarked by the experience of caste discrimination based upon color" (1965, p. 15). Subsequent policy responses led to the creation of special preschool training programs and self-awareness movements that attempted to renovate these young,

but pathological, selves. Recurrent research findings have supported this argument while often suggesting that the programs have been unsuccessful or that the problem is more serious than anticipated (Clark 1965; Pettigrew 1964; Havelick and Vane 1974; Hauser 1971).

Yet this evidence is far from conclusive; in fact, a number of significant studies argue that either there is *no difference* in level of self-esteem between inner-city Black youth and their White counterparts or that *Whites* have lower levels of self-esteem (Coleman et al. 1964; Rosenberg 1965; Soares and Soares 1969; Zirkel and Moss 1971). These findings often go unnoticed and unanalyzed, with few attempts to reconcile the apparent contradictions. A number of authors emphasize, however, that discrepancies can be accounted for by differences in methodology, rationale, operationalizations, or instruments (Greenberg 1970; Zirkel 1971; Greenwald and Oppenheim 1968). In any case, the empirical issue with attendant policy implications remains unresolved.

The purpose of this chapter is to examine data concerning the self-appraisals of Black and White urban students in a major northern city. More specifically, we will: (1) describe the relationship between self-appraisal (self-derogation), race, and socioeconomic status, and (2) examine *qualitative* differences in type of self-reference by race.

METHOD

Our data were collected during a survey administered at three metropolitan high schools, an upper-middle socioeconomic status suburban school and two widely separated city schools, one largely Black and the other largely working-class White. The purpose of the survey was to collect baseline data on drug use among students in target schools for use in evaluating neighborhood drug programs.

The population for the study was defined as the junior classes of high school. The sample was selected from all students enrolled in American history or any similar social studies or health

---

[1]Strictly speaking, the argument presented here does not deal with the ego in a Freudian sense. More to the point (lest Whitehead turn in his grave!), the term *flat ego* is employed only to expressively connote the variety of pejorative terms used by various writers to convey what they think are the effects of racism and classism on the self-conceptions of youthful minority members. These selves have variously been referred to as abnormal, pathological, depressed, poor, self-contemptuous (Bloom and Hess 1965), inadequate (Dreger and Miller 1960), and damaged (Grambs 1965); the term *deflation* was in fact employed by the Ausubels in 1963.

class at the junior level. Since these topics were required of all students by the state, it is considered that no bias existed in assignment to the class, and thus each class can be viewed as a cluster sample from the population. From the lists of all these classes, random samples of classes were drawn by assigning a number to each class listed in a particular school and then selecting classes by means of a random table of numbers. Selection continued until an N of approximately 200 students was obtained, requiring four to six classrooms in each of the three schools. This technique resulted in a sample which was in effect age controlled, at about 16 years. The procedure was followed in May 1971 and repeated in December 1971 with another cohort of juniors. The sample of students drawn in this fashion approximates a random sample of students at this age level in these schools, although technically precise generalizations can only be made to the junior classes. For the purposes of this analysis, the two groups are analytically combined.

The survey questionnaire was administered to the students in the classes in the sample. Administration time for the questionnaire was approximately 35 minutes or one full class period. Since the purpose of the survey was to obtain self-reports bearing on possible deviant behavior, considerable care was directed toward establishing rapport between students and administrators in the test situation. The purpose of the survey was fully explained. The regular teachers were absent from the room while the protocols were distributed and completed. Since the schools were relatively segregated, we matched race of interviewers with racial categories predominant in each school (Ledvinka 1971).

Overall, 1149 students responded to the questionnaire. At Time I, 187 protocols were obtained in City High White, 185 in City Black, and 216 in Suburban High. At Time II, 213 were obtained in City White, 143 in City Black, and 205 at Suburban. The class attendance rate was approximately 85 percent although attendance at City Black at Time II dropped to about 66 per-

cent. These figures are difficult to analyze because of varying statements by school personnel regarding the exact number of students who were expected to be present in class. The response rate to the questionnaire for those present was very high (99 percent plus).

OPERATIONS

The self-instrument utilized was the Kuhn Twenty Statements Test (TST) (Kuhn 1960; Kuhn and McPartland 1954; Spitzer, Couch, and Stratton 1972). The TST is an open-ended device that permits use of a variety of interpretative coding procedures. Substantial data are available concerning the validity and reliability of this test (Spitzer and Stratton 1966).

The rationale for the TST suggests that group life is the fundamental source of self-perception, i.e., self-concept is the product of social interaction. Unlike previous attempts to examine the relationship between race and self-esteem that relied largely on nonphenomenological approaches including checklists, closed indexes, and contrived experiments, the TST allows us to enter the dialogue of the self and examine the source of particular modes of self-perception.

The modified version of the TST employed here consisted of one page of the questionnaire with 15 numbered lines following a single question at the top of the page:

There are fifteen numbered blanks on the page below. Please write fifteen answers to the single question "Who am I?" Answer as if you were giving the answers to yourself—not to somebody else. Write your answers in the order that they occur to you, don't worry about logic or "importance." Go along fairly fast; the time for this section is limited.

The perspective from which this item was developed asserts that this question elicits statements about the self made to self, that people are conscious, aware of self-meanings, and can put that meaning into words.

Kuhn's theory, symbolic interaction in general and the various perspectives employed by those who argue that Blacks *ought* to have nega-

the data. The interpretation which seems most accurate indicates that the increased share of respect and importance given to Black women has not affected the dominant position of males in Black society. The outstanding consequence, however, has been the acceptance by Black children of the feminine role as a worthy one. This acceptance has led some researchers to believe that Black children are overpowered by feminine influence. Instead, it may suggest that the experience of the Black child permits a greater adaptability in social situations.

References

Baruch, G. K. "Maternal Influences upon College Women's Attitudes Toward Women and Work." *Developmental Psychology* 6 (1972): 32-37.

Bieber, I., et al. *Homosexuality: A Psychoanalytic Study.* New York: Basic Books, 1962.

Biller, H. B. "Father Absence, Maternal Encouragement and Sex-Role Development in Kindergarten-Age Boys." *Developmental Psychology* 1 (1969): 87-94.

Biller, H. B. "Fathering and Female Sexual Development." *Medical Aspects of Human Sexuality* 5 (1971): 126-138.

Biller, H. B., and Zung, B. "Perceived Maternal Control, Anxiety and Opposite Sex Preference among Elementary School Girls." *Journal of Psychology* 81 (1972): 85-88.

Broom, L., and Glenn, N. D. *Transformation of the Negro American.* New York: Harper & Row, 1965.

Connell, D. M., and Johnson, J. E. "Relationships Between Sex-Role Identification and Self-Esteem in Early Adolescence." *Developmental Psychology* 3 (1970): 268.

Doherty, A. "Influence of Parental Control on the Development of Feminine Sex-Role and Conscience." *Developmental Psychology* 2 (1970): 157-158.

Elkin, F., and Handel, G. *The Child and Society: The Process of Socialization.* New York: Random House, 1972.

Hannerz, U. *Soulside: Inquiries into Ghetto Culture and Community.* New York: Columbia University Press, 1969.

Harrington, C. C. *Errors in Sex-Role Behavior in Teen-Age Boys.* New York: Teachers College Press, 1970.

Hetherington, E. M. "A Developmental Study of the Effects of Sex of Dominant Parent on Sex-Role Preference, Identification, and Imitation in Children." *Journal of Personality and Social Psychology* 2 (1965): 188-194.

Hetherington, E. M. "Effects of Father Absence on Personality Development in Adolescent Daughters." *Developmental Psychology* 7 (1972): 313-326.

Hetherington, E. M. "Girls Without Fathers." *Psychology Today,* February 1973, pp. 47-52.

Hetherington, E. M., and Deur, J. L. "The Effects of Father Absence on Child Development." *Young Children* 26, no. 4 (1971): 233-248.

Hill, R. *The Strengths of Black Families.* National Urban League, New York: Emerson Hall Publishers, 1972.

Holter, H. *Sex Roles and Social Structure.* Oslo, Norway: Universitetsfortaget, 1970.

Joshi, A. K. "Sex-Role Preference in Preschool Children from 5 Subcultures of the United States." *Dissertation Abstracts International* 30, no. 2-B (1970): 5120.

King, K. A. "A Comparison of the Negro and White Family Power Structure in Low Income Families." *Child and Family* 6 (1967): 65-74.

Kogan, K., and Wimberger, H. C. "Sex Role and the Relative Status in the Relationship of Mothers to Children." *Perceptual and Motor Skills* 29 (1969): 782.

Mack, D. E. "Where the Black-Matriarchy Theorists Went Wrong." *Psychology Today,* January 1971, pp. 24, 86-87.

Miller, W. B. "Lower-Class Culture as a Generating Milieu of Gang Delinquency." *Journal of Social Issues* 14 (1958): 5-19.

Moynihan, D. P. *The Negro Family: The Case for National Action.* Washington, D.C.: U.S. Department of Labor, U.S. Government Printing Office, 1965.

Munger, M. B. "Sex Differentiation in Preschool Children: Sex-Typical Toy Preferences and Knowledge of Peer's Sex-Typical Toy Preference." *Dissertation Abstracts International* 32, no. 6-B (1971): 3646.

Mussen, P., and Rutherford, E. "Parent-Child Relations and Parental Personality in Relation to Young Children's Sex-Role Preferences." *Child Development* 34 (1963): 589-607.

Rainwater, L. "Crucible of Identity: The Negro Lower-Class Family." *Daedalus* 95 (1966): 172-216.

Rosenkrantz, P.; Vogel, S.; Bee, H.; Broverman, I. E.; and Broverman, D. M. "Sex-Role Stereotypes and

Self Concepts in College Students." *Journal of Consulting and Clinical Psychology* 32 (1968): 287-295.

Rutherford, E. "Familial Antecedents of Sex-Role Development in Young Children." *Dissertation Abstracts International* 25 (1965): 4252-4253.

Scanzoni, J. H. *The Black Family in Modern Society.* Boston: Allyn and Bacon, 1971.

Sternglanz, S. H., and Serbin, L. A. "Sex-Role Stereotyping in Children's Television Programs." *Developmental Psychology* 10 (1974): 710-715.

TenHouten, W. D. "The Black Family: Myth and Reality." *Psychiatry* 33 (1970): 145-173.

Thompson, N. L., Jr., and McCandless, B. R. "It Score Variations by Instructional Style." *Child Development* 41, no. 2 (1970): 425-436.

Ward, W. D. "Patterns of Culturally Defined Sex-Role Preference and Parental Imitation." *Journal of Genetic Psychology* 122 (1973): 337-343.

West, D. J. *Homosexuality.* Chicago: Aldine Publishing Co., 1967.

Concluding Statement

There are some consistent themes that are evident in all the selections in this book of readings. While any one chapter may not explicitly address each of the themes, it is remarkable that such a diverse set of authors, writing on such a diversity of topics, would evidence unanimity on so many points. The first theme is a healthy skepticism of existing research findings. Many of the chapters contain critiques of existing research methodologies and of the assumptions which have guided variable selection and data interpretation. These reasoned critiques of existing paradigms should provide readers with many tools for analyzing existing research and for conceptualizing future research. A second theme is the recurrent recognition that so little is known about cultural differences. While certain cultural differences have been identified in some areas, such as language, the implications for education based upon those differences are only beginning to be understood. We obviously feel that the identification of cultural differences and the developing of educational programs which recognize and value those differences is a vital task. A final theme is the recognition that myths or stereotypes do not exist because of research on inner-city children. Rather, myths are a product of a society whose political, economic, and social structures are served by their existence. Unfortunately, we did not have conference presentations that analyzed in detail the relationships between the current social order and child psychology, sociology, and education. Such work is a prerequisite to fully understanding the implications of the cultural difference position.

In conclusion, it is our position that for too long we have "blamed the victim." We know that large numbers of inner-city children fail in school. However, we reject simplistic analyses of the cause of that failure. We hope that the readings in this book will stimulate research workers and practitioners in all fields related to children to reexamine their own values and assumptions and to act based upon that reanalysis.

APPENDIX
Demythologizing the Inner-City Child
Conference Presentations
Urban Life Center
Georgia State University
March 25, 26, and 27, 1976

Dr. Asa G. Hilliard
Dean, School of Education
San Francisco State University
San Francisco, California

The Education of "Inner-City" Children

Dr. Harriette McAdoo
School of Social Work
Howard University
Washington, D.C.

A Reexamination of the Relationship
Between Self-Esteem and Race
Attitudes of Black Children

Dr. John R. Stabler
Dr. James Zeig
Department of Psychology
Georgia State University
Atlanta, Georgia

Children's Racial Membership
and Their Perception of Racially
Related Stimuli

Ms. Valora Washington
Interdisciplinary Program
   on Young Children
Indiana University
Bloomington, Indiana

Learning Racial Identity

Dr. Pamela Trotman Reid
Department of Psychology
Philadelphia Community College
Philadelphia, Pennsylvania

Are Black Children Feminized by
Maternal Dominance?

Dr. Arthur C. Littleton
Academy of Urban Service
St. Louis, Missouri

The Role Models and Vocational
Aspirations of Black Elementary
School Children

Dr. Leon Jones
School of Education
Howard University
Washington, D.C.

The Inner-City Child and the
Uniform Education for All Myth

Dr. Muriel Berkeley
Department of Social Relations
The Johns Hopkins University
Baltimore, Maryland

School Resources

Dr. Russell W. Irvine
Department of Educational Foundations
Georgia State University
Atlanta, Georgia

The Explicit and Implicit Meaning of *Demythologizing the Inner-City Child*

Dr. Jualynne Dodson
School of Social Work
Atlanta University
Atlanta, Georgia

The Myth of Cultural Deficiency

Dr. Mary T. Dailey
College of Arts & Sciences
Florida Agricultural and Mining
    University
Tallahassee, Florida

A Fallacy in the Social Sciences

Dr. John R. Dill
Professor, Department of Psychology
City College of New York
New York, New York

Toward a Developmental Theory of the Inner-City Child

Dr. Murray Krantz
Department of Educational Psychology
University of Wisconsin
Milwaukee, Wisconsin

Multiple Model Programming and the Advent of the Urban Superchild

    and

Dr. Marce Verzaro-Lawrence
Colleges of Home Economics and
    Education
University of Tennessee
Knoxville, Tennessee

Dr. Richard O. Hope
Department of Sociology
Morgan State College
Baltimore, Maryland

Reassessment of the Inner-City Child's Self-Concept

Dr. Sadie A. Grimmett
Institute for Child Study
Indiana University
Bloomington, Indiana

Information Processing Competencies of Inner-City Black Children: Knowing How to Know the World

Dr. Robert Cervantes
D.C. Development Assoc., Inc.
San Antonio, Texas

Self-Concept, Locus of Control and Achievement in Mexican-American Pupils

Dr. Andre Joseph Department of Psychology University of Texas Austin, Texas	Social Class, Race, and IQ: Facts, Fictions, and Findings
Dr. Leonard I. Jacobson Department of Psychology University of Miami Miami, Florida	Intelligence—Myth and Reality

Dr. John W. McDavid
Department of Counseling &
   Psychological Services
Georgia State University
Atlanta, Georgia
   and
Dr. Larry E. Greeson
Department of Educational Foundations
Georgia State University
Atlanta, Georgia
	Sociomotivational Factors and
	the IQ Test Performance of the
	Inner-City Child

Dr. Albert Reese Department of Educational Foundations Georgia State University Fort Benning Campus Columbus, Georgia	W.E.B. Du Bois, A Man for All Seasons
Maj. Hector Dueno Georgia State University Fort Benning Campus Columbus, Georgia	The Educational Conflict Between W.E.B. Du Bois and Booker T. Washington
Capt. Thomas Francis Schmitz Georgia State University Fort Benning Campus Columbus, Georgia	The Educational Theory of W.E.B. Du Bois: A Culturally Pluralistic Alternative
Ms. Phyllis J. Dukes Department of Psychology University of Michigan Ann Arbor, Michigan	The Effects of Early Childrearing Practices on the Cognitive Development of Infants
Ms. Pat Nesmith Early Childhood-Special Education Georgia State University Atlanta, Georgia	Infant Day Care: Effects on Development

Ms. Carol Edwards
Ms. Jamila Jones
Black Educational Process, Inc.
Atlanta, Georgia

Concerns in the Development of
Curricula for Black Children

Dr. Ellen G. Jacobs
Dr. Jeffrey L. Derevensky
Department of Education
Concordia University
Montreal, Quebec

Changing Teachers' Perceptions:
A Look at the Inner-City Child's
Environment

Dr. Buckley Barnes
Department of Curriculum and
    Instruction
Georgia State University
Atlanta, Georgia

Myths Preservice Teachers
Believe about Inner-City Children

Dr. Robert D. Ruth
Department of Sociology
Davidson College
Davidson, North Carolina

Pygmalion Revisited, or The
Effects of Teacher Socialization
and Occupational Concerns upon
Sharing Their Attitudinal
Conceptions of Inner-City Children
and Parental Demands for Community Control

Dr. Janice E. Hale
Department of Education
Clark College
Atlanta, Georgia

Play as a Mode of Cultural
Expression and Its Relationship
to Learning among Black
Inner-City Children

Ms. Michele Rubin
Clark College/Academy Theatre
Arts-in-Education Program
Atlanta, Georgia

When Is Gladys Knight and the Pips
Arts-in-Education? or Children Teach
the Teacher How to Teach

Dr. Linda Mixon Clary
Former Professor of Education
Augusta College
Augusta, Georgia

Language Development and the Inner-
City Child: Comparing Syntactic
Characteristics and Reading
Approaches

Dr. Mona Farrell
Department of Education
Concordia University
Montreal, Quebec

Reading Achievement in Three
Canadian Inner-City Grade One
Classrooms

Ms. Lynn Harmon
Department of Early Childhood Education
Georgia State University
Atlanta, Georgia

The Training of Day Care Staff
and Parents

Ms. Barbara Ann Pearson
Department of Reading-
   Early Childhood
Chicago State University
Chicago, Illinois

Contextual Influences of Home
and School on the Reading
Achievement of the Inner-City
Child

Dr. John Hollomon
Dr. Gloria Zamora
Dr. Ronald Lacoste
Dr. Pamela Werton-Dalton
Department of Early Childhood Education
The University of Texas
San Antonio, Texas

Demythologizing the Inappropriateness
of Behaviors of Inner-City
Children in Classroom Situations:
An Analysis and Interpretation

Ms. Lois Clark
Department of Early Childhood Education
Georgia State University
Atlanta, Georgia

A Collaborative Parent Education
Program

Dr. Miller Boyd
Academy of Urban Service
St. Louis, Missouri

Racial Misidentification and
the Self-Concept of Preschool
Children

Dr. Harvey A. Moore
Department of Sociology
University of South Florida
Tampa, Florida

Examining the Flat Ego: A
Problem of Self-Concept, Race,
and Social Myth

Dr. Charles E. Billiard
Department of Curriculum and
   Instruction
Georgia State University
Atlanta, Georgia
   and
Dr. Joan M. Elifson
Humanities Division
Atlanta Junior College
Atlanta, Georgia
   and
Dr. John W. Rubadeau
Department of English
Lincoln Memorial University
Harrogate, Tennessee

Attitudes about Nonstandard
Dialects Can Be Changed

Dr. George E. Temp
The Educational Testing Service
Atlanta, Georgia

Myths about Testing and Inner-
City Children

Dr. Joanne R. Nurss
School of Education
Georgia State University
Atlanta, Georgia

An Attempt to Reduce Test Bias
in Readiness Tests

Dr. Clifford Carter
Department of Counseling
Georgia State University
Atlanta, Georgia

Testing and the Black Child

Ms. Mae Armster Christian
Director, Teacher Corps
Atlanta Public Schools
Atlanta, Georgia

Teacher Preparation

Dr. Lucretia Payton
Department of Curriculum and
    Instruction
Georgia State University
Atlanta, Georgia

An Encounter with Reality

Dr. Charlie Mae Edwards
Director of Staff Development
Atlanta Public Schools
Atlanta, Georgia

Staff Development

Dr. Anna Obong
Associate Professor
Department of Educational Sociology
University of Pittsburgh
Pittsburgh, Pennsylvania

The Sociology of Inner-City Children